BISHOP GORE

AND THE

CATHOLIC CLAIMS

NIHIL OBSTAT.

LAMBERTUS NOLLE, O.S.B.
Censor Deputatus.

IMPRIMATUR.

GULIELMUS PRAEPOSITUS JOHNSON,
Vicarius Generalis.

WESTMONASTERII,
die 22 Aprilis, 1905.

BISHOP GORE

AND THE

CATHOLIC CLAIMS

BY

DOM JOHN CHAPMAN, O.S.B.

LONGMANS, GREEN, AND CO.
39 PATERNOSTER ROW, LONDON
NEW YORK AND BOMBAY
1905

PREFACE

SOME seventy years ago certain minds in the Established Church were earnestly intent on searching out a *via media* in religion, *i.e.* a middle ground between what was known as "Roman" doctrine and mere Protestantism. In this voyage of discovery the pioneer was the illustrious Newman. To this he for some years devoted his talents, his learning, and his best energies in the hope of finding security for himself and others in the bosom of the Church in which he had been brought up, and which he still cherished as a mother. The result of it all was that he found he had to give up the task as hopeless, and he sought safety for his own soul by submitting to the Holy, Roman, and Catholic Church. His secession might well have proved the death-blow to all *via media* enterprise; yet since that day others have ventured upon it with hope that they might succeed where he failed. Of these not the least distinguished by his ability, learning, and religious earnestness is Dr. Gore, who has recently been enthroned as bishop of the newly-founded Anglican See of Birmingham. His book on Roman Catholic Claims appears to be in great demand. It is mainly an attack on the positions we hold. And there can be little doubt that many of the unwary who read it will regard it as conclusive against our claims, and not a few are being held back who would otherwise feel disposed to follow Newman into the Catholic Church. For the sake of these, and for the benefit of those who come to us in an inquiring frame of mind, the "Reply" of Dom Chapman, O.S.B., to the "Roman Catholic Claims" will be found most useful. Within the space of 124 pages it supplies an answer to the leading questions which are raised in that book. I commend it, therefore, to the clergy and laity of my diocese as a sufficient statement and vindication of Catholic doctrine on the points it deals with. And I can assure the gifted and learned author that we shall all appreciate the scholarly way in which he has accomplished his task, and the kindly, courteous, and temperate tone he has maintained throughout.

✠ EDWARD,
Bishop of Birmingham.

Oscott College,
    May 8th, 1905.

TO THE RIGHT REV. C. GORE, D.D.

My dear Lord Bishop,

    Your appointment to the new Anglican see of Birmingham has been contemporaneous with the publication of a sixpenny edition of your book on " the Roman Catholic Claims." To many this popularising of an attack upon Catholicism at the moment of your assumption of a title which has been borne for half a century by a Catholic Bishop must necessarily appear to be a challenge.[1] I am quite sure that you had no such intention, and the tone of your sermon and speech on March 2nd, on the occasion of your enthronement, would alone suffice to show that you have not entered upon your new duties in a spirit of hostility to Catholics, or to anyone else, but just in that spirit of friendliness to all, which those who know you would have expected you to show.

    Nevertheless your sixpenny book is a challenge, and it is unavoidable that someone on the Catholic side should pick up the glove which you have thrown down. I am glad to be the one to do so, although I dislike controversy, although I have much work in hand that I do not enjoy thrusting aside, although I have no confidence in my own competence for the work, because I know I can approach the task as one who has both affection and respect for yourself personally. I, at least, shall not assume that you have opened your mouth for the first time among us at Birmingham with an offensive proclamation of enmity, and others might reasonably have taken a different view. I am sorry if it should seem that I am welcoming you to Birmingham with disagreeable remarks ; but I am writing a reply, not an attack. I am glad to have the opportunity of saying how much good I know you will wish to do, and how much of it will necessarily have the sympathy of Catholics. Because I necessarily complain of the negative views expressed in your attack on our religion, it is not to be supposed that I forget how much of the

---

[1] *It is described on the cover as the work of the " Bishop-Designate of Birmingham," and " ninth edition " is not found outside. The above was written before your letter, denying that you had challenged anyone, appeared in the Birmingham papers of March 20th.*

Christian Truth you hold, and how much you labour in the Christian cause against the common enemies—ignorance, indifference, unbelief, and sin. You defend a great part of our position with weapons borrowed from our armoury. You have access to many whom we cannot reach. Our message is delivered but to the few in this country, for we are few, and few will listen to what we say. It is well for our country that so much of the truth is proclaimed outside the Church. I am more inclined to rejoice where you happen to accept a truth, than to be annoyed where you happen to deny one. I have avoided with care the impulse to snatch here or there a controversial victory on some minor point, and I have resisted the temptation to make my pamphlet lively or amusing at the expense of politeness. I have tried to imitate the tone of moderation which you have employed everywhere but in your eleventh chapter. I have tried to treat you, not as being a mere controversialist, but as a seeker after truth. That you must be merely a seeker, and not an authoritative teacher, is obvious. Your own Church claims no infallibility, indeed she has (it is said) no definite views. You have not her authority for what you say. What you think to be "Catholic Doctrine" is so in your opinion, and in that of sometimes but few others. I take it therefore that your views are advanced without any absolute certainty on your own part, and that they demand, at most, a respectful attention on the part of others. For this reason you cannot refuse to consider the other side. You have not yet considered it enough. I can say this without impertinence or conceit. You know one side of the question. I also know it well. If I was young when I left your communion, I had heard its ecclesiastical politics discussed around me from my cradle. Most of my best friends have been, or are, clergymen of your Church.

But there is another side, and you seem to know it very little. You show constantly that you do not understand how Catholics comprehend their own dogmas, and you naturally do not anticipate Catholic tendencies and feelings. A little more knowledge would, I know, have removed a good deal of prejudice. I do not reply to you as an authorised teacher, or as an official champion, nor is the Catholic Church answerable for the way in which I present her teaching. I write rather as a friend answering—unsolicited— the difficulties which you have encountered—I am afraid I must say, the difficulties you have sought out. If my answers are unsatisfactory, there are, in most cases, plenty of other answers to be given: I have given those which seemed to me the most satisfactory or the most obvious.

I must further add that I have necessarily been obliged to write in haste, for it would not do to postpone the publication of this reply. Consequently I have written currente calamo, *using notes of my own, old publications of my own, with scarcely any reference to books beyond those needed for the verification of quotations. I am conscious that the result would have been different had I had time for special study and for slow composition. But such as the work is, I think it will be a sufficient answer, in spite of any inaccuracies I may have been unable under the circumstances to avoid. My reason for so much confidence is that I am not only on the side of the Catholic Church, but of the vast majority of theologians and scholars. Of dogmatic theology, in fact, there is extremely little outside the Catholic Church. On the patristic questions with which I have dealt, I have nothing to fear, for patristic study has always been mainly in the hands of Catholic scholars.*

I wish to apologise beforehand for any misrepresentations of your views which I may have set down without malice. I have tried to interpret you in the most Catholic sense your words seemed capable of bearing. I wish to emphasize agreement, not difference. We serve one Master. You serve Him in your way, we serve Him in His way.

I am always yours sincerely,

fr. JOHN CHAPMAN, *O.S.B.*

. ERDINGTON ABBEY, BIRMINGHAM,
    Lent, 1905.

CONTENTS

CHAPTER I

BISHOP GORE AND THE CATHOLIC CLAIMS

CHAPTER I

THE *VIA MEDIA* AND THE CATHOLIC CLAIMS

(I reply to Dr. Gore chapter by chapter)

OTHERS often see us more clearly than we see ourselves. Bishop Gore begins his book with the complaint that the English Churchman " is constantly liable to be told—and to be told from very opposite quarters—that if he were only 'logical' he would join the Roman Church." A warning that comes from opposite quarters is likely to be of importance. If it were urged by Catholics alone— that is to say by half the Christians in the world—it is clear that the members of the comparatively small Anglican communion would be bound to give it some attention. But it is well known that the same note is sounded by others. The more Protestant sects assure the English Churchman that he is on the way to Rome. Less fiercely, yet even more securely, the agnostic declares that there is no logical resting-place in Christianity short of that bourne to which all roads proverbially lead, and from which admittedly few travellers return. It is, indeed, a commonplace with all those who are outside the Anglican communion to condemn her position as illogical.

It is certainly well-advised of Bishop Gore to place in the forefront this remarkable objection, if he feels himself able to prove it mistaken. In this first chapter he meets it indirectly, by denying that the " Roman " position is logical, for it is too logical. He quotes a striking and well-known passage from J. Mozley's reply to Newman on Development, in which that eloquent writer points out that the early heretics were logical in their own way : "The Arian, the Nestorian, the Apollinarian, the Eutychian, the Monothelite developments, each began with a great truth, and each professed to demand one, and only one, treatment for it. All successively had one watchword, and that was 'Be logical.'" Now their fault was obviously not in their desire to be logical, but in the incompleteness of their premises. They started with only half of the truth, and they concluded to a falsehood. Bishop Gore thinks he can trace three instances of this " one-sidedness" in the Roman Church, not in questions of doctrine, but beyond the sphere of theology proper.

1. Protestantism is individualistic, Romanism absolutist. The Anglican Church attempts to preserve the balance between these two extremes, so Dr. Gore thinks. It seems to me that the type of "absolutism" should rather be Calvinism; for individualism we may take Wesleyanism or Evangelicalism. Does the High Church system combine the two? It appears to fall short of both. System and government exist in theory, but in practice vanish into thin air. This naturally leaves the individual free to develop fads, which, however, scarcely represent the individualism contemplated by Dr. Gore. In the Catholic Church "absolutism," in the sense of organised government, is as perfectly developed as anything can well be in this imperfect world, and far more perfectly, it seems, than can be accounted for by natural means. But what of individualism? The answer is ready. The Catholic Church has a way of growing Saints which is shared by no other communion. They are not turned out all alike as by a machine, but have the most startling individualities, so that the world has constantly counted them as mad. In a well-managed garden flowers are healthier, larger, brighter, than in the fields, precisely because their idiosyncrasies are protected, encouraged, assisted to develop. And for this reason "individualism" in the truest sense flourishes far more luxuriantly in the enclosed garden of the Catholic Church than in the uncultivated meadows and woods without. Perhaps, if Dr. Gore thinks otherwise, it is because he has not had a good opportunity for judging.

2. "The case is just the same with authority and private judgment."

"The extremes are represented by a dogmatism which crushes instead of quickening the reason of the individual, making it purely passive and acquiescent, and on the other hand by an unrestrained development of the individual judgment which becomes eccentric and lawless just because it is unrestrained. If there is much of this latter extreme in modern life, there is also in the Roman Church a great deal of the former" (p. 5).

This is all very odd. The matter with which "dogmatism" professes to deal is nothing else than revealed truth. The whole question with regard to "dogmatism" is whether the dogmas propounded are true or not. If they are true, if they are revealed by God, the more of them the better,—they are no matter for the individual judgment. If they are merely human arguments, probabilities, guesses, then their imposition by human authority would evidently be an appalling evil. Now the Catholic Church professes to define the point at which certainty with regard to revealed truth has arrived, and to decide controversies when the discussion is complete, and the case is properly presented. So far under anathema. Beyond this there may be points closely connected with defined dogma; here the theologian must tread with caution. Sometimes a critic who is not a theologian shows himself rather too free, and is pulled up by authority. At once the whole anti-Catholic world shrieks, "Tyranny!" Such warnings are not delivered with an infallible voice—let us grant that it may be that in a few cases a condemnation has been ill-judged, and has tended to "crush" reason; such over-caution on the part of ecclesiastical authority is invariably a protection of the common opinion of the community against the daring of the individual. If it is unfortunate, it is anyhow exceedingly rare. In fact, any condemnation at all is uncommon, precisely because the territory is so completely mapped out and the dangerous ground is so narrow. Beyond this the theologian is free.

The "via media" of Anglicanism seems to be rather to obliterate definitions, all but a few, and to leave even these somewhat uncertain. Shall she accept three creeds or only two? four councils or six? the Bible only, or also the authority of the Church? the teaching of the first three centuries, or of the first six or sixteen? In other words, the rule of faith itself is left doubtful, and the Church of England does not claim the right to define it. Consequently she assigns a sphere to dogmatism in fundamentals, without being able to set a limit to that sphere, leaving to private judgment a large field wherein it can neither speculate with freedom nor submit with reason to the recognised voice of God. Hence the contrast between Anglican and Catholic theological writers. So long as the decisions of the Church are safe the Catholic is free to argue as he will, provided he gives good reasons for his views. Consequently he writes boldly and with no anxiety. The Anglican, on the other hand, scarcely ventures to deduce or to infer. He cannot submit where he has no certainty, yet when he rebels it is without confidence. He has developed for his own use a characteristic formula: "May it not be that . . . ?" It is a formula which, in the matter of the relation of my soul with God, would, I confess, afford me no consolation whatever.

3. "The doctrine of the sacraments has without a doubt been preached and accepted in such a way as to lead to their being treated as charms or substitutes for personal spiritual effort; and on the other side the sufficiency of faith has been proclaimed in a way that made men ignore the necessity of the sacraments." I do not profess to know where, when, and by whom the sacraments have been treated as charms. In the Catholic Church the greatest of the sacraments is protected from becoming a "charm" by the universal custom of prefacing it by sacramental confession. The latter, as Dr. Gore is well aware, implies sorrow for sin and the determination to do better. The system of habitual confession has arrived by degrees at its present perfection, and forms the most wonderful system for making men good, —for inducing "personal spiritual effort,"—that the world has ever known. Dr. Gore has, unfortunately for him, not had the opportunity of experiencing how the sacramental teaching of the Catholic Church works in practice. But I am glad to recognise that he brings no accusation against the Church in general, and I do not think he means to find fault here. He does not even venture, for obvious reasons, to prefer the actual practice of the English Church. He only claims that she has an ideal synthesis of "the belief in the validity of sacramental grace and the necessity for the responsive action of faith, which the providence of God has made it our special responsibility to maintain." Now this means nothing else than that the bishop has a theory of his own on this subject. It is well known that he holds that confession of mortal sins is not obligatory, though highly beneficial. Some mortal sins may be confessed and others held back, and the penitent is not bound to answer the questions of the confessor. This original and, I suppose, unique system (in which the confessor ceases to be a judge of the dispositions of the penitent, and will obviously be

liable to give absolution for sins confessed and apparently repented, while the penitent has other unrepented sins which he does not choose to mention) was fully described by Dr. Gore in the *Guardian* some years ago, but has certainly not met with much acceptance in the Anglican Church. It is consequently not necessary to discuss it. But I cannot help saying that an *ex hypothesi* unnecessary absolution, demanded from a confessor who has not the whole case before him, might seem to be really regarded somewhat as a "charm"; for the confessor can never be sure of the suitability of the advice he gives, nor can the penitent have assurance of the validity of the absolution he receives beyond his own conviction of the sufficiency of his contrition. However this may be, at all events it is not the official or obligatory system of the Bishop's own communion.

The three points with which we have been dealing are excellent instances of the vague statements in which Dr. Gore is in the habit of indulging. No proof is forthcoming, and they are naturally refuted by mere contradiction — *quod gratis affirmatur, gratis negatur.* From these three points he infers that, "speaking broadly," the Roman Church is not heretical, but a one-sided development. Bishop Gore is studiously moderate, but he has been unable to make good even this moderate complaint, by speaking ever so broadly. He continues his "broad" generalities on p. 7: "Broadly it is very easy to justify this view of the Roman Church." So it seems. Would it be equally easy to justify it by a narrow inspection? The question is not answered, for we find next some very wide statements, which are worth examining, for the very reason that they have no dogmatic bearing.

(*a*) "Each race has had in the Catholic Church its own particular function. It was the function, for instance, of the Greek race with its peculiar intellectual subtlety and philosophical power to bring out into clear light the 'treasures of wisdom' which lay hid in Christ, to grasp and enunciate the principles of the Incarnation and the Trinity—in a word, to be the theologians of the Church."

Of "the Greek race," strictly speaking, this is wholly untrue. Probably Dr. Gore means "the Greek-speaking races," thus lumping together the whole complexus of diverse nationalities, whose polite language was Greek. Yet even so, of all the Fathers, none is so much the type of intellectual subtlety as the African Augustine; none is more severely practical and anti-philosophical than Chrysostom, the characteristic product of Antioch, the capital of the East.

(*b*) "In theology proper the Roman Church has been by comparison weak, but her strength lay in the gift of government." If the Church of the city of Rome is alone meant, no individual town except Alexandria can be preferred to Rome in theology. If, however, the whole West is meant, the statement is still quite untrue. The Greek-speaking Christians in the early centuries were far the more numerous, and yet the body of Latin Fathers are at least the equals of the Greek Fathers in "theology proper." "The faculty of empire passed from Pagan to Christian Rome transformed in purpose and motive, but fundamentally the same." It is, on the contrary, curious to notice that ecclesiastical organisation was not only much earlier developed in the East than in the West, but that it was more complete, and more powerful. Of the great bishops, it was not the Italian, but the Egyptian Patriarch who exercised the most effective tyranny over his subordinates.

(*c*) "The primary conception of her (Rome's) unity becomes that of unity of government." This is undoubtedly a libel. History plainly shows that her primary conception of unity has always been unity of faith, of which, however, unity of government is a necessary condition in practice.

(*d*) The Church's dogma is "to the Easterns the guide in the knowledge of God, to the Westerns it is the instrument to subdue and discipline the souls of men." Surely it is impossible to rise to the knowledge of God, except by the subduing and disciplining of the soul.

(*e*) "It is no longer enough to conceive of the Church as the Catholic witness to a faith once for all delivered. She must be the living voice of God, the oracle of the Divine Will." Excepting the expression "Divine Will," where "Intellect" seems rather to be intended, I can accept this as a statement of Catholic doctrine. But to what can Dr. Gore possibly take exception in this view? He admits that the Church is the Catholic witness to a faith once for all delivered, but he appears to deny that she is the living voice of God. A witness implies a voice; so it remains that he objects to the word "living," or to the words "of God." Does he mean that the Church is the living voice of man, and nothing more? Surely not. Then he must mean that she is the dead voice of God. In this case she is a dead witness. Dr. Gore explains: "Just as the strength and security of witness lies in the comparison and consent of independent testimonies . . . ." (thus, according to Dr. Gore, the individual has to compare a multitude of testimonies of the dead witness,

and has no other guide,) "so the strength of authoritative oracular utterance lies in unimpeded, unqualified centrality, and Christendom needs a central chair of truth, where Divine authority speaks and rules." But this is not the Catholic theory. The Pope is not an inspired oracle. He simply gives voice to the belief of the Church. We believe that the Church is a living witness, Dr. Gore thinks she is an inanimate witness, whose testimony needs to be collected by historians. How this theory works in practice, we shall see later.

On pp. 16 and 17 Dr. Gore formulates his case on behalf of Anglicanism. "We do not find on examination that we fail to comply with any of the conditions of Catholic communion which the ancient and undivided Church recognised." So they find, but most other Christians think them mistaken in this supposed discovery. Are they sure that they are right? And how very hard to be thus driven to study ancient history in order to determine whether one is within the Church or not!

"We cannot in the face of history treat the claims of the Papal See as tenable or just." The reasons for this will be considered in chapters vi. and vii. "History forces us to recognise in the Roman claims the main cause of the schism of East and West." History, that is, as read through Anglican spectacles. Historians usually recognise the Eastern Emperors, and not the Popes, to have been answerable for the schism.

"On the other hand, we see in the ancient and undivided Church a coherent system of beliefs and institutions and practices, which has been continuous under the development of Rome and in the traditions of the East, and which is richer and fuller in possibilities of life than either the one or the other taken apart. To this richer and completer life of the undivided Church we make our appeal. From it we would start afresh."

This modest proposal to make a fresh start is hardly very complimentary to the Anglican Church.

The "richer and fuller life" referred to is somewhat vague; but the Anglican can choose what centuries he pleases in which to dig for antiquities, and he will have a large assortment of traditions at hand for the new commencement. Whether any unanimity in the final result can be expected is another matter. But for myself, I must beg to disagree with the Bishop on the fundamental question. I am not prepared to grant that the ancient Church was on the whole preferable to the modern. There were giants in those days: yet there is a fulness and richness in the Church of the twentieth century which was lacking in the fourth or fifth. I do not believe that the Church of God has been continually deteriorating ever since her foundation, but I believe that she has a divine life which increases in her without end. Take only one point: the sanctification of the individual Christian. How moral and ascetical theology have been perfected! We possess a science of direction, a wealth of spiritual literature, a pliant but systematic method, which are our inheritance from a long, coherent, and venerable past. The Catholic tradition does not grow faint and pale with the lapse of years, but as age succeeds age, the tradition is but clearer and fuller, richer and more fruitful. But I cannot wonder that Dr. Gore, from the standpoint of Anglicanism, should cast a regretful glance at those ancient days to which he appeals. He has not experienced the blessing of belonging to the Church of to-day, else he would read the past with different eyes. He would love the ancient Church life better than he does now, because he would understand it better: but he would also, I think, perceive that the later we live, the richer is our inheritance from the past, and the more perfect the development of the present.

But Bishop Gore finds consolation in the progress which his Church has made already. It is true, and I also am most thankful for it. Only I greatly fear that the Broad-Church movement has made at least as much progress, and in an opposite sense. But I venture to think that his note on p. 18 is altogether mistaken. If in the early years of the tractarian movement the eyes of the party were much turned towards Rome, Dr. Gore thinks that this has long since ceased to be the case. Of course the first rush of converts after the conversion of Newman was but a passing phenomenon, followed by a thin, though ever-flowing stream. But the truth is, that the movement of the whole English Church has been unceasingly Romewards. The Evangelical party is no longer of any importance, while, such as it still is, it has moved so far with the times that the material aspect of its churches and its services is far more 'ritualistic' than was that of the 'advanced' churches as late as 1845. Meanwhile the leaders of the vanguard and the skirmishers have gone forward apace. When I became a Catholic in 1890, reservation of the sacrament was unheard of, except in a few convent chapels. Incense was uncommon. I remember being quite startled to hear that these two points had in five or six years come to be regarded as necessary to the fulness of Church life. Every year the habits borrowed from Rome or from the Catholic Middle Ages become more ingrained. What were once watchwords of the advanced line are ever becoming part and parcel of the ordinary High Church claims. The old High Church positions are now held by the moderates. It seemed a few years ago that the high-water mark had been reached, and that no further forward movement was possible. It had become common to hear of black Masses, rosaries, devotions to St. Joseph and to the Sacred Heart, but one venture had still been felt too bold. At length Canon Everest wrote a book, *The Power of the Keys*, to defend the Primacy of St. Peter, and Mr. Spencer Jones followed it up with a defence of the Papal claims. It is as yet but a number of extremists who have fully accepted this new point. But it was in accordance with the analogy of the past that some should dare to push ahead, and grasp this truth also; and it is similarly in accordance with ~~been~~ that, where a few have led ~~a forlorn hope,~~ many should follow through the breach. The countenance given by Lord Halifax o Mr. Spencer Jones, and the energetic propaganda in the United States carried on by the *Lamp*, are gradually producing their effect. Already the 'geographical' theory is disappearing, according to which Anglican chaplains on the Continent are schismatics, while the Catholics in England are regarded in the same light, though their state of schism ceases if they should cross the Channel. The 'Branch' theory has become old-fashioned, and an elaborate and elusive, but in some ways far more tenable, theory has taken its place. According to this view the Church of England is a province (or rather, two or more provinces) of the Catholic Church, which has no doubt exceeded its powers in self-government, and has become enslaved to the State. But it has never become actually committed to heresy, in spite of the heresies which have been, and are, permitted to its children, through the loss of discipline. It is natural that these provinces should have been excommunicated by the rest of the Church. Some regard this separation as a misunderstanding, which will be removed when the Church of England can show herself in her true light, after a thorough reformation. Others add that, since the separation took place, the rest of the Church has exaggerated certain doctrines, notably that of Papal infallibility. Others more reasonably are prepared to accept all that the Church teaches. Others again, more reasonably still, admit that the Church of England deserved to be cut off, and that she is therefore in formal schism. They hold, however, that it would be wrong for themselves to leave her, (though they forbear to judge those whose consciences bid them do so), because they hope for a day of reconciliation and of corporate reunion. The old unreasoning horror of Rome has to an extraordinary extent passed away. In 1867 it was quite natural for a distinguished writer like Charles Kingsley to use language about the Church, which would now hardly be tolerated in the *Rock* or the *English Churchman*. In 1888, when Dr. Gore's book first came out, its chief claim to attention was its great moderation of attitude, for that date. Since then the trend of things has been ever Romewards, and Dr. Gore's ninth edition is likely to be regarded by many of his friends as quite a savage attack!

I think, then, that the Church of

England as a whole, (apart from the Broad party), is moving steadily and corporately Romewards. The very fewness, comparatively speaking, of conversions has tended to ensure this result, though, of course, I hold that no one could have the right to remain outside the true Church for this reason. Some day, perhaps, there will come a greater exodus, and I suppose that the exodus will be likely to be so much the larger as it is further off. Of corporate reunion there do not seem to be any hopeful signs, for the mass of the nation, while it grows less hostile to Catholic ideas, at the same time grows more indifferent with regard to them and to religion in general.

These remarks on Dr. Gore's first chapter must suffice. He has not by his broad generalities succeeded in showing the Catholic Church to be a one-sided developement. We have now to see whether he is able to present an Anglican theory which can be regarded as logical.

CHAPTER II

THE UNITY OF THE CHURCH

THE divisibility of the Church is the cardinal doctrine of Anglicanism, and its most fundamental heresy. There are signs, as I have just been saying, that it is being relinquished by the most advanced school, but then this school professes to hold "Anglicanism" in holy horror. Dr. Gore, on the contrary, is the apologist of what was, when he wrote, very high, but now is moderate, Anglicanism; and he naturally puts forward this essentially modern doctrine in the place of honour in his work, immediately after the programme which occupies his first chapter.

He poses the objection to be answered with admirable conscientiousness :—

"It is a question often asked of English Churchmen, 'In what sense do you believe in *one* Holy Catholic Church? You do not claim that the English Church is of itself and alone the whole Church; you admit the Roman and Eastern branches to be equally with your own parts of the Church; that is to say, you admit permanent and apparently radical divisions in the Church in matters of doctrine no less than of government, and yet you say the Church is one. Surely you are here giving words an unreal meaning. Surely the Romanists can call the Church 'one' in a much more intelligible sense. What they mean by Church unity is plain and tangible. Their Church is 'one.'"

The answer given by Bishop Gore to this serious difficulty is neither plain nor tangible, but in the highest degree involved and elusive. He seems determined at all events to avoid the reproach of being too logical.

"Primarily," he says, "the Church is the Spirit-bearing body, and what makes her one in heaven and paradise" [note this curious High Church distinction] "and earth is not an outward but an inward fact—the indwelling of the Spirit—which brings with it the indwelling of Christ, and makes the Church the great 'Christ-bearer,' the body of Christ."

So far, I suppose, all Christians agree. It is not to be denied that the union of each Christian soul with Christ, through the operation of the Holy Ghost, causes a mystical and invisible union between them all. But this cannot be the unity of which we are in search, for it evidently can only include those who are in a state of grace, since those who are divided from Christ by mortal sin have forfeited the gift of His indwelling. There are indeed ultra-Protestant sects who do not blink at this result, and who include in the Church only the good, or, with Calvin, only the elect. But of course I do not suspect Dr. Gore of meaning this, and yet I confess that I fail to extract any other meaning from his words. He seems, indeed, further on to be referring to some indwelling of the Spirit in the Church in her corporate capacity : " She is one because she alone of all societies of men possesses a supernatural indwelling presence and relation to God in Christ." But it would be unkind to credit him with the natural meaning of these words. The indwelling of Christ in the Church as a society implies that she is already a society. It cannot, therefore, be the cause of her unity, but only a sequence of it. So that here also Dr. Gore must be speaking of the sanctification of each individual.

On page 30 a clue to his meaning seems to appear. He anticipates an objection :—

" ' But then,' it will be said, ' you are saying that Church unity is primarily invisible.' We reply that even at this primary stage the unity is external as well as internal. . . . This inward life depends on outward means. Without baptism, without the 'laying on of hands,' which gives the gift of the Holy Ghost in His personal indwelling, without the Eucharist, without absolution, we cannot have or retain the inward gift ; and those external channels depending, as we all acknowledge they do, on the apostolic ministry, connect the inward life of the Church at once with her outward organisation. . . . It is only through this visible organisation that God has covenanted to give us this invisible life."

We were led to expect something about visible unity, but not a word is forthcoming. We are told, indeed, that the invisible unity depends on an outward organisation, but it does not appear that this outward organisation need have any unity of its own besides the transcendental unity which invisibly binds its individual members to Christ. And in fact we know that Dr. Gore does not believe that unity in the external organisation is necessary. He has consequently given no reply to the objection which he himself proposed. In other words, he confesses that the Church has, in his view, a spiritual and invisible unity only. He differs from the extreme Protestants in that he teaches, even to exaggeration, the necessity of an outward organisation, that is to say, of a visible Church, but a visible Church which need have no visible unity. Surely he is here, indeed, giving words an unreal meaning. A visible Church which is visibly divided is rather to be spoken of as several visible Churches. It will be perfectly logical for him to speak of one invisible Church, and this all Christians agree in admitting ; but he cannot logically use the singular number when speaking of the Church on earth, which he maintains to be visible and to have a necessary organisation. He is the more bound to be logical on this point because he refuses to "treat the Church on earth as a separate unity." Nothing, therefore, can be clearer than that Dr. Gore dogmatically denies all visible unity to the Church on earth. How could he avoid this when he holds that the Anglican, the Eastern, and the Roman 'branches,' though mutually excommunicating one another, yet are all parts of the visible Church?

I do not propose to refute this Dogma of the Divisibility of the Church out of Holy Scripture. It is obvious that nothing can be quoted in favour of divisibility. On the other hand, every text which can be cited for the visibility of the Church assumes its visible unity. The Fathers are fond of proving the necessity of unity in the Church on earth by its foundation on Peter. But I leave the Bible alone, because, as Dr. Gore will fully admit, the Bible, apart from the Church's interpretation, is liable to very various uses, and is claimed as the support of every heresy. But the ancient Church speaks on this question with no uncertain voice. I challenge Dr. Gore to find any of the Fathers admitting the possibility of a divided Church. There is no doctrine on which they are more insistent or more full than the question of visible unity. It is hardly necessary, I hope, to remark that the Fathers do not follow Dr. Gore in refusing to treat the Church on earth as a separate entity. Sometimes they may speak of the Church *sensu adæquato*, as embracing all who ever have belonged to it or ever will, as in the passage quoted by Dr. Gore from St. Augustine on page 34 of his book. Modern Catholics sometimes speak in the same way. But this is somewhat uncommon. It is usual, with the Fathers as with us, to mean by the Church the visible Church on earth ; and it is certain that Dr. Gore himself almost always uses the word in this sense.

Theologians demand for the Church a threefold visible unity.

1. The primary unity is UNITY OF FAITH, for the Church is the living witness throughout all ages to the faith once delivered. On this point the Fathers are unanimous and clear. Perhaps the most obvious to refer to is St. Irenæus, who in the second century appealed to the consentient witness of a continuous and universal Church against the heretics of the time. To refer to other Fathers is supererogatory, as I suppose their doctrine on this subject is not denied. This is the "symbolical bond." To break it is the sin of heresy.

2. This unity of faith is guarded and demonstrated by UNITY OF INTERCOMMUNION, which is called the liturgical bond. To break it is the sin of schism. Against heretics this unity is pointed out to be a fact, as a means of demonstrating that unity of faith which heresy dares to break. But against schismatics, such as the Novatians and Donatists, the necessity of communion with the Church was the point to be proved. It is therefore in the writings of St. Cyprian, St. Pacian, St. Optatus, and St. Augustine against these schismatics that we find this doctrine most fully argued and illustrated, though it is indeed taught by all the ancients with one voice. Before passing on, let us hear a few words from St. Cyprian in the third century, from whom the rest were so fond of borrowing :—

"The Church which is one and Catholic is not severed or divided, but is indeed *joined together and connected by the glue of bishops adhering to one another*" (*Ep.* 66, 8).

"There is one body of Christ and one Church of His, and one faith and one people joined together into a solid unity of body by the glue of concord. *The unity cannot be severed, nor can the one body be divided by a separation of its component parts, nor by the laceration of its vitals be torn to fragments.* Whatever departs from the womb will not be able to live and breathe apart, and loses the substance of salvation" (*De Unit. Eccl.*, 23).

"And does anyone believe that this unity which comes down from the Divine unchangeableness, and which coheres in heavenly sacraments, can be severed in the Church? . . . Whoso holds not this unity, holds not life and salvation" (*De Unit. Eccl.*, 6).

If I were Dr. Gore, I should not like to be thus addressed by this illustrious Saint and Martyr.

St. Cyprian, in these passages, is meeting a schism in his own Church of Carthage. He employed the same writings over again, and the same arguments, against the Novatians, who seemed for a moment to be about to split the Catholic Church into halves. The later argument against the Donatists is similar. Optatus and Augustine point to the one Church throughout the world, from which the Donatists in Africa have divided themselves. Let Dr. Gore think a little what arguments he could possibly bring against the Donatists from his own position. So far as I can see, he would have nothing with which to reproach them. As far as faith was concerned they were not heretical, though they were inclined to some mistaken opinions, which were afterwards condemned. They held the old sees of Africa, in most cases with an unbroken succession from the former Catholic bishops, and in almost every city they had a direct continuity with the anterior Catholic life. They were so large a majority in Africa, that they could reasonably claim to be a national Church. They declared that it was not they who had fallen away, but that the rest of the Church had cut itself off from unity by sin. Two principal arguments were brought against them by the Catholic writers, and neither of them is accepted by Dr. Gore. The first I have already stated : the Donatists were in Africa only—the universal Church was their judge, and they were outside it. They had no right to claim the name of Catholic, and they were separated from unity. The second argument was their separation from Rome, the centre of unity, and from all the ancient Apostolic foundations.[1]

3. The third kind of unity is UNITY OF GOVERNMENT—the subjection of the faithful to the same pastors. This is called the "hierarchical bond." We have seen it described by St. Cyprian as the subjection to bishops who are connected together by the glue of concord. The complete and fully developed hierarchy of the Church has the

[1] Bishop Gore speaks of the Donatists on p. 129 : "Be it remembered that the Donatist body in Africa was not constituted by a reform of a national Church, but was as distinct a schism *from* the Church as ever took place." In other words, the Donatists retained the Catholic rule of faith, and the whole Catholic system of faith and practice. They did not "reform." The Anglicans, as an actual fact, fell into varied and incoherent heresies, and gave up most of the habits as well as teachings of Catholic life. (I am not saying that they committed themselves irrevocably to their new ways and views.) The contrast is unfortunately not in favour of the moderns. Dr. Gore continues : "and that the Donatist body held itself the only true Church of the world." In other words, the Donatists held to the cardinal doctrine of the unity of the Church, in spite of the absurdity of supposing it to exist only in Africa and in the little community of *Montenses* who surrounded the Donatist Pope at Rome. It never struck them to suppose that two rival communions could possibly be part of one visible Church ! Tichonius, the one Donatist scholar, seems indeed to have taken a view somewhat similar, but he was singular in his opinion, and was attacked most violently by the protagonist of his sect, Parmenianus. St. Augustine could not understand why Tichonius did not become a Catholic, for he did not see how Tichonius could admit that the Church throughout the world had not fallen away, and yet could think he had a right to remain a Donatist.

successor of St. Peter at its head, and consequently this third form of unity centres in the Pope. The historical development of the hierarchy will be spoken of in chapter vii.; at present it is sufficient to point out that in the second century we find Rome quite clearly the centre of unity. I will not dwell upon this, as I do not think Dr. Gore would deny it. It is, however, impossible to pass over the point urged repeatedly against the Novatians by St. Cyprian, that in communicating with an Anti-pope they separated themselves from the Church. He could not have said this with regard to communion through error with the wrong one of two rival claimants of any other see. Against the Donatists it was repeatedly urged that they could not be the whole Church, for they had not the chair of Peter. They were so conscious themselves of this fatal weakness in their position that they actually set up a private Anti-pope in Rome itself. But there at least they had no continuity with the past; and their claim only brought ridicule upon them. St. Optatus opposes to them the real succession of bishops in the chair of Peter, and St. Augustine is never tired of plying them with this same argument.

These three bonds of unity, then, the symbolical, the liturgical, and the hierarchical, are all, according to the Fathers, indispensable to the visible Church on earth. One faith, one communion, one spiritual government. The unity of faith is primary and fundamental. It should naturally issue in the union of all believers in one fellowship, without which the unity of faith cannot survive. To guard in its turn the unity of fellowship and communion, the hierarchical bond is needed, on account of the tendency to quarrel which we have derived from original sin. This is a logical theory, and it answers to the facts of history.

Let us now contrast with it Bishop Gore's conclusion :—

"Enough has been said to show that the true idea of Church unity makes it to consist primarily in the derivation of the life of the Spirit from Christ, down the channels of his organised society; not in subjection to an external hierarchy centering in the Pope."

We have seen that Catholic theologians do not make hierarchical unity the primary unity, so here Dr. Gore is tilting against a windmill. He himself makes invisible unity the only unity, so far as he has explained his views in this chapter; and I must remind the reader that it is a unity which includes no sinners, while it surely embraces all Christians outside the visible Church, who are in good faith because they know no better, and are doing their best to follow the law of Christ. Nay, I do not think Dr. Gore will be so harsh as to deny that even heathens may have that indwelling of the Holy Ghost without which no man can be saved, and that they may so be unconsciously united to Christ. Unless this be granted, it is hard to see how it can be maintained that God truly desires all men to be saved, and that He places the means of salvation within the reach of all. The result of Dr. Gore's chapter is this: We come to him to hear in what sense the Church on earth is one, and he tells us: "Oh, I cannot consent to treat the Church on earth as a separate entity!" And then he describes for us a unity which, though a true one, yet is anyhow wholly outside the sphere of our present discussion, and which is not only wholly invisible, embracing both the saints in heaven and the saints not yet born, but which even must be allowed to include many heathens within its field. This unity is not a peculiarly Anglican tenet, but is the common belief of all Christians. There was no reason why it should enter into the discussion at all. But at least we have reached the knowledge that Dr. Gore has nothing to tell us about the unity of the Church on earth, that he is at open war with the Fathers, and that they condemn him in no measured language.

CHAPTER III

THE AUTHORITY OF THE CHURCH

A.

THERE is a great deal in this chapter which expresses the truth remarkably well, and comparatively little with which a Catholic will disagree. Unfortunately, Dr. Gore has not understood the Catholic position, and, as usual, tilts against a good many windmills. It will be best to begin with a few short extracts, which contain doctrine which I cordially accept :—

"The Church is not only, through her sacraments, the household of grace: she is also the 'pillar and ground of the truth': she has the authority of a divinely authorised teacher, and her legislative enactments in the sphere of truth, no less than of discipline, have a divine sanction" (p. 37). "Whatever is new to Christian theology in substance, is by that very fact proved not to be of the faith. This is a commonplace of patristic theology, and it is admitted by the modern Roman Church" (p. 38). The Church "is not a perpetual oracle of divine truth, an open organ of continuous revelation: she is not so much a 'living voice' as a living witness to a once spoken voice" (p. 40).

It would be simpler to say for "She is a voice," "She has a voice," the voice of a witness, not of a revealer, of truth. All this is Catholic doctrine, correctly expressed. Unfortunately, Dr. Gore does not continue with the same clearness of statement. He knows that all this is held by the Catholic Church of to-day, yet he is under the impression that she has other teaching which is inconsistent with it. Now Catholic theology is enshrined in scholastically argued tomes and in orderly text-books, composed by highly trained professional theologians. If Dr. Gore was more familiar with this voluminous literature, he would recognise the rashness of supposing that any obvious inconsistency could remain unnoticed and undiscussed by acute logicians, who are only too ready to find each other in the wrong. I fear that Dr. Gore has not even taken the obvious precaution of reading carefully at least one of the many standard treatises *De Ecclesia*. Yet some knowledge of the ordinary teaching of the Church, such as he would have gained by this study, would have helped him very much towards the composition of a refutation of that teaching. We will examine his indictment.

1. We are agreed that the Church is a living witness to a revelation which is final, from which nothing can be taken away, and to which nothing can be added. This is the fundamental principle, which is to be the touchstone of all that follows.

2. But Dr. Gore thinks that we actually hold many new doctrines which were unknown to antiquity; and that to support them we are obliged to look upon the Church as an oracle, having an inspired oracular voice at Rome. This evidently flatly contradicts our fundamental principle, and every Catholic theologian would deny and denounce such a doctrine. If any careless Catholic writers, in the heat of controversy perhaps, have ever used words which might be twisted to yield such a sense, such authors must be interpreted according to the certain teaching of the Church to which they belong—or, if not, they must be treated as dangerous, and approaching near to heresy. That any respectable Catholic writer has ever actually stated the theory of an inspired Church or Pope in the way Dr. Gore puts the theory, I do not believe. But at least this much is certain : nothing whatever of the sort will be found in any approved theological treatise, for in these accurate wording is a necessity.

3. But we do hold that doctrine *develops*. The development of dogma is not a weapon of controversy invented by the genius of Cardinal Newman, as many of our Anglican brethren seem to think. It is a portion of the teaching of the Church, and is found in every treatise *De Ecclesia*, in that part which is entitled *Tractatus De Traditione*. I will not, however, describe the doctrine in the words of modern theologians, for Dr. Gore wishes for earlier evidence. He has himself appealed to St. Vincent of Lerins, and to St. Vincent of Lerins he shall go.[1]

[1] By a strange coincidence, Fr. Rickaby has used this same formula in his excellent *Development, thoughts on Bp. Gore's 'R. C. Claims,'* pp. 12, 13. Dr. Gore says, p. 56, note 2 : "The whole chapter should be read.

Commonitorium, xxiii. (55.) "But perhaps someone will say, 'Will there then be no progress of religion in the Church of Christ?' There will, indeed, the greatest progress. For who is so full of hate to men, so hated by God, as to attempt to deny this? (*Nam quis ille est tam invidus hominibus, tam exosus Deo, qui istud prohibere conetur?*) But in such wise, however, that it should be a true progress of faith, and not a change. Now it belongs to progress (*profectus*, growth) that each thing should be increased into its own self; it belongs, on the contrary, to change, that one thing should be turned into another. Therefore the intelligence, knowledge, wisdom, both of a single man and of the whole Church, must grow, and make great and enormous progress by the advance of ages and centuries, but only within their own nature, that is to say, in the same teaching, the same sense, and the same meaning."

Nothing could be clearer than this exposition by an ancient Father of the doctrine of development. Let us at once take an example. The tradition of the Church from the beginning held that the Father

The earlier part speaks of the growth of 'religion' as a whole. It grows as a child to manhood. Each limb increases in size, but no new limb is added, or old one removed. Then it passes to the development of the *doctrine* of the Church." What Dr. Gore means by "progress of religion" I do not know. What St. Vincent meant was precisely the same as progress of dogma. There is no change of subject in the chapter. The very first words of it announce the theorem : "But perhaps someone will say," etc. This objection is brought against the exposition in the previous chapter of the words : "Depositum custodi," "Keep that which is committed to thee," and the chapter on development is in reality an explanation of the last words of that exposition : "Let that be more clearly understood by thy instruction which before was more obscurely believed. By thee let posterity rejoice in comprehending what antiquity without comprehension venerated. Yet teach the same that thou hast learned, so that thou say not new things while saying newly (*ut cum dicas nove, non dicas nova*)."

is God, the Son is God, and the Holy Ghost is God, and that there is (as reason also assures us) only one God. Unaided reason, however, would not succeed in harmonising these two dogmas of Three who are one God. It was not sufficient that the Church should faithfully and ceaselessly bear witness to the original deposit of truth in the same words, but it was imperative that she should be able to judge of the various heresies which distorted the truth in one way or another, and answer the questions that emerged from time to time. As we find the dogma exposed in St. Augustine's *De Trinitate*, it is the result of three centuries of discussion and profound thought. In the Middle Ages the philosophical elaboration of the mystery, as we have it in St. Thomas Aquinas, is again the conclusion of laborious contests of scholastic disputants, and the outcome of the application of Aristotelianism to philosophy. But without the guidance of the Holy Spirit in the Church there is no knowing what the resultant dogma might have turned out, if, indeed, there had resulted a dogma at all ; for it is, perhaps, more likely that the disputes would not have issued in any common agreement. Thus the persistent witness of the Church to what she received from the Lord has ensured the identity of the teaching throughout, under the varying form of its expression, while her authority has been divinely assisted to decide what was in harmony with the original deposit and what was not. Yet it is probable that a Christian of the year 100 would have been puzzled by the Athanasian Creed ; he would have held implicitly all that it enunciates, but the fierce antitheses might well have surprised and shocked him. Judged by the standard of the first four Œcumenical Councils, scarcely a single ecclesiastical writer of the first three centuries is orthodox in expression.

Let us continue the quotation from St. Vincent :—

" The religion of souls should follow the nature of bodies, which, though they unfold and develop their years in the process of time, yet remain the same that they were. There is a great difference between the flower of boyhood and the maturity of old age ; but those who become old men are the same who once were youths ; so that although the condition and circumstances of one and the same man are altered, yet he is one and the same nature, one and the same person. The limbs of babies are small, those of youths are big, but they are identical. Children have the same number of members as men ; and if there be any which are produced by maturer age, they are already there after the manner of seed (*iam in seminis ratione proserta sunt*), so that nothing new is brought forth in the old which was not already latent in the child. Wherefore without doubt this is the legitimate and right rule of progress, this the proper and perfect order of growth, that the tale of years should ever unfold in the more advanced those parts and forms which the wisdom of the Creator had previously formed in the young. But if the human species should be changed into some likeness other than its own nature, or if something should either be added or subtracted from the number of members, the whole body must perish, or become a monster, or at least be weakened. So also the teaching of the Christian religion ought to follow these laws of progress ; that is to say, that it should be consolidated by years, enlarged by time, uplifted by age (*annis scilicet consolidetur, dilatetur tempore, sublimetur ætate*), but yet remain incorrupt and undefiled, and be full and perfect in all the proportions of its parts and in all its members (so to speak) and senses, admitting further no permutation, no loss of its own character, no variation in its outline."

This passage is extremely remarkable in its anticipation of the modern theory of evolution. It has been inevitable that this universal category should be applied to-day to religion as to all other subjects. Dr. Gore is naturally not unconscious of this, and he has added as an appendix a paper on Evolution, which he read at a Church Congress, pp. 203–11. Evolution was in the air before Darwin; and Hegel first, and then Newman, were in the field long before Herbert Spencer. But we have been hearing a writer of the year 434 comparing dogma to an organism, and working out the likeness with success. The growth of which this ancient Father speaks takes place, like that of an organism, by nutrition, with assimilation of what is suitable, and rejection of what is harmful: the Church feeds upon the current ideas of the time; she digests them by the disputes of her theologians; part is assimilated, part is cast out. For instance, at the beginning of the third century, a whole gang of heresiarchs invaded the Church of Rome, Theodotus, the leatherworker, and his crew of " adoptionists " on the one hand, and on the other, Sabellius, and other Monarchians, who in various ways obscured the distinction of persons in the Holy Trinity. In the fourth century the Arians attacked the root of the doctrine, while some forms of semi-Arianism seemed to make three or two gods. In the course of the conflict the Church learned to understand her own mind far more clearly, and to be able to reply to questions which had not been asked in earlier times. She had assimilated the terminology of the philosophers. She had begun to possess a philosophy of her own. She had learned to speak the language of her time, and to think with its most cultured thought. This training was needed for the position she was to hold in the world after the Emperor's conversion. And ever since, the same process of growth by assimilation and rejection has continued. It is the divine assistance (not inspiration) which enables the Church to choose rightly, to obtain growth without change. An organism has this power of assimilation and rejection because it is living. The Catholic Church, by possessing it, shows that she lives. The Greek schism has lost the function of nutrition. She rejects error, indeed, for she rejects even food, and is incapable of receiving anything. She has life no longer, but is as if a mummy. The Anglican Church, on the other hand, has the greatest facility for accepting new doctrine of any kind, but she lacks that faculty of discrimination which is the mark of life. She has no power of rejecting. She receives like a pail; she does not feed and digest like an organism.

We have heard the Catholic view; now we must hear Dr. Gore.

" According then to the older and really Catholic view, the later Church can never know what the early Church did not. She can never have substantially clearer light about the intermediate state, for example, or the relation of the departed to the living, or the 'treasury of merits,' or the position of Mary, than the Church of the second century had. The revelation receives no augmentation, and what for our discipline was left obscure at first must remain obscure, according to God's providence, till our fragmentary knowledge becomes complete in the Day of Light."

This is only a half-truth. It is right to say that "revelation receives no augmentation," if addition is meant, just as an organism cannot receive addition. But we have seen that St. Vincent would deny, and vehemently deny, that it cannot grow. Similarly, it is certain that "the later Church cannot know what the early Church did not," if by this statement new facts are excluded. But the later Church ought to comprehend the meaning of her own dogmas, their application, their richness and fulness after centuries of meditation, with a perfection which was as little needed as it was impossible to the early periods. Again, it is true that she "can never have substantially clearer light" about any doctrine; for "substantially" seems to imply a change of substance. But she can have, we will say, a "very much" clearer light on all that has been revealed. Now I imagine that Dr. Gore will not really quarrel with this corrected version of his words. I suppose he will rather shift his ground, and admit the teaching of St. Vincent, and perhaps even my exposition of it. Only then he will have another position to fall back upon, namely, that the modern Church has added to dogma and not merely understood it better. This is a far more consistent and intelligible ground to take up, and, of course, it cannot be completely answered except by defending the entire theological system of the Catholic Church, and by tracing the historical development of every separate dogma. Yet it is possible to meet the objection on two more general grounds: first, then, it is unhistorical; secondly, it is impious.

1. It is unhistorical. In the first four centuries dogmas seem to have developed much more quickly than afterwards, but the evidence is too obscure for us to be able to follow the course of their growth with any ease. Fortunately the later evolutions, which are precisely those to which Dr. Gore objects, can be traced with comparative certainty. It can be shown that they have not grown by borrowing from without, from heathen ideas, from philosophical speculations — that popular devotions have not been allowed to influence dogma, but that every least growth has been subjected to the most painful scrutiny, to prolonged discussion, and has only passed muster when proved beyond all doubt to be a necessary sequence of what was already of faith. Scholastic theologians are distinguished by their rigid conservatism. Dr. Gore does not realise this simply because he has not had leisure to study Catholic theology and its history.

2. The objection is impious. If Dr. Gore is right, the Church has gone wrong. If the developments of dogma up to the sixteenth century were to a large extent mistaken, then the Church has fallen from truth; the infallible Guardian of the faith has failed in her trust. She has not kept the deposit, as St. Vincent said and believed she must and would. Nearly all that Dr. Gore rejects as unwarranted addition was common to East and West before the consummation of the schism. It must be allowed, then, that the whole Church fell away simultaneously. Even where it may be that the Western Church now stands alone (as with regard to the Papacy), it is bad enough if Dr. Gore has to own that a great part of what he admits to be the Church is in grievous error. He will perhaps say that he does not consider these novelties to amount to heresy, they have not been formally condemned by a council of the whole Church. It is, no doubt, condescending of Dr. Gore to allow this much, but it will not avoid the difficulty. For the question is not what Dr. Gore thinks heresy, but what the Eastern and Western Church has formally

defined to be heresy. They declare heretical the denial of many of those points which he regards as novelties. If these points are additions to the faith, the fact that they are imposed as conditions of communion is all important. Additions have then been made by the Church which are insisted upon by her as being of the first consequence. The Church has consequently been found wanting in her chief office, and can clearly make no claim to divine guidance. The assistance which was promised to her has not been forthcoming. We gather that He who promised was wanting either in good faith or in power.

This is the painful result of such a rejection of the claims of the Church. But Dr. Gore will ask how we are to escape from this unpleasant conclusion, for he is sure that the teaching of the modern Church is full of additions to the original deposit of faith. It is of no use for me to refer him, as I have already done, to the endless volumes which have been written upon the subject. If he has not yet studied them, but has contented himself (as I suppose he has, perhaps from want of time) with the perusal of a few books of controversy, I cannot well expect him now to begin, still less can every reader of his book be expected to verify his broad statements. For this reason I am afraid it is unavoidable that we should consider a few important instances of development.

To begin with, Dr. Gore himself has chosen some examples, as we saw : the intermediate state, the relation of the departed to the living, the "treasury of merits," the position of Mary. We will take them in order :

   1. The "intermediate state" is a euphemism for what Catholics call Purgatory. How does Dr. Gore know that there is an intermediate state ? Protestants hold that there is no such thing, but that all who are not damned go at once to heaven when they die. Dr. Gore makes on page 26 a curious distinction between heaven and Paradise, but he has not explained what he means by Paradise. I cannot criticise his views on the intermediate state, for I do not know what they are. As for those of the early Church, the primary fact is that they are exceedingly hard to trace. It appears that Holy Scripture was not found to be very distinct on the question, and consequently we find the most puzzling diversity of view and the most disconcerting conjectures where the Fathers deal with eschatology. We may find an otherwise severely orthodox Father holding with Origen that the devil will be saved. It is easier to understand why many bishops were harsh enough to refuse absolution and communion, even in the hour of death, to those who had committed certain heinous crimes, when we remember that it was a widely spread opinion among Catholics, that, while all heathen and heretics must necessarily go to hell for ever, yet all the orthodox, however criminal and unrepentant, must necessarily be saved, "yet so as by fire." In other words, all bad Christians were to go to temporal punishment, not to eternal—to purgatory, not to hell ! Dr. Gore is of course aware that the custom of praying for the dead has been constant from the earliest ages of the Church. It was certainly not thought that they were still in a state of probation ; it remains that they were believed to be in a state of purification.[1]

[1] Bishop Gore quotes Dr. Salmon to the effect that "Purgatory had not got beyond a 'perhaps' in St. Augustine's

Now I quite agree with Dr. Gore that on this particular point there has been no development, for the Church has not had occasion to define anything beyond what was the universal belief in the very earliest times, viz. that "there is a Purgatory, and that the souls which are detained there are helped by the prayers of the faithful, and especially by the acceptable sacrifice of the altar."[1] I suppose Dr. Gore believes this much. On the other hand it is not to be doubted but that the writings of theologians have thrown some little light on this mysterious subject. At least the beautiful treatise of St. Catharine of Genoa is most suggestive, though of course she does not speak with authority.

2. "The relation of the departed to the living" is again a question where it would appear that no progress has been made, so far as official definitions are concerned, since (say) the fifth century.[2] Then

day." This is an error: St. Augustine did not doubt the existence of a Purgatory, but he was uncertain whether the text of St. Paul about trial by fire (1 Cor. iii. 13) should be understood of Purgatory or not.

[1] The Council of Trent uses these words in the *Decretum de Purgatorio*, Sess. xxv. The only important definition on the subject is in Sess. vi., Can. xxx: "Si quis post acceptam justificationis gratiam cuilibet peccatori pænitenti ita culpam remitti, et reatum æternæ poenæ ita deleri dixerit, ut nullus remaneat reatus poenæ temporalis exsolvendæ vel in hoc sæculo, vel in futuro in purgatorio, antequam ad regna cælorum aditus patere possit: anathema sit."

[2] I have said the fifth century, because it would seem that there was a considerable development before this time. In the New Testament we do not expect to find prayers to the martyrs who had not yet suffered, but as saints multiplied the devotion to them grew up. It was certainly universal and very prominent throughout the fourth century, but material is lacking for any systematic account of its growth up to this stage. Develop, however, it must have done, for it is inconceivable that when saints were few the devotion should have

as now, and as much as now—I am inclined to think more than now—the faithful were in the habit of yet reached the height which we find in the fourth and fifth centuries.

But Dr. Gore has chosen the cultus of the saints as a crucial instance of a false development, a deterioration, in the "mediæval and modern" Church, giving his reasons for this view in the Appendix, pp. 207, 208. He there says: "It (the Roman development) is the result of an over-reckless self-accommodation to the unregenerate natural instincts in religion. I confine myself to one significant illustration of the latter proposition. I mean the development of the cultus of the saints in its mediæval and modern form. It is written on the face of Church history that this has resulted from Christianity accepting, not without preliminary protest, but finally even with enthusiasm, what is simply an almost universal phenomenon of untaught natural religion all over the world. If you travel in many a Buddhist, or Mohammedan, or Christian country, you see the same facts; the same devotion gathering round the tomb of departed saints, who are regarded as intercessors or mediators, and as patrons of particular places, or trades, or classes, and are approached with divine, or semi-divine, homage," and so on. Of the last words I say nothing, for I do not wish to suppose that Dr. Gore really accuses Catholics of paying divine honours to the saints. I assume that this expression is meant for the other religions of which he speaks. But the rest of the sentence is a good instance of his utter recklessness of statement. To say that saint-worship is an "almost universal phenomenon of untaught natural religion" is indeed an astonishing assertion! No instances are given but two. Of Mohammedanism it is certain that it borrowed the idea of a cultus of saints from Christianity. As to Buddhism, I do not know whether it has or has not been influenced by Christianity in this point. I understand that such an influence in general is to some extent a matter of uncertainty. However this may be, it is anyhow unimportant in view of the influence of Confucianism, the religious part of this system being ancestor worship. But what other religions have shown a tendency to saint-worship? It is not found, so far as I know, in the degraded religions of Oceania, nor in the antique superstitions of the American continent, nor in Africa, nor in Brahmanism, nor in the ancient religions of Persia, Egypt, Babylonia, Assyria. I speak generally:

asking the Saints to pray for them, in full confidence that God would see to it that their words should not be unheard. The only advance that I can think of is that the doctrine of the beatific vision has since then been more philosophically treated, and that it is therefore now more clearly taught that it is in God that the Saints see the

there may be traces, but there is no marked prevalence. The demi-gods of the ancient Greeks are not instances, for they were not revered as holy persons nor as benefactors of the human race, nor as intercessors. There was no cultus of Harmodius and Aristogiton, nor of Lycurgus or Solon, of Socrates or Pericles. Nor in the remains of the old Roman religion was there any tendency of this kind, unless Romulus is an instance. Yet Dr. Gore says, "The half-converted masses passed into the Church with this dominant instinct of hero-worship still in them—with the dominant demand for mediators and objects of worship less high and holy than God." What the first part of this sentence may mean, I have really no idea. The official worship of the emperors, and the provincial assemblies in connection with the cultus of Augustus and Rome, these are surely not manifestations of "hero-worship"! Yet I do not see what else can be referred to. The latter part of the sentence is the well-known Protestant jest, that the saints of the Catholic Church are nothing but the old false gods with new names. This has a grain of truth in it. No doubt the cultus of some saints may have been even encouraged for the purpose of supplanting some deep-rooted superstition. But the notion that "saint-worship" is a corruption due to the old idol-worship is a libel which St. Augustine long ago suggested as an objection, and refuted. I will conclude by quoting a short passage of his: "But our martyrs are not our gods, for we know that the martyrs and we have both but one God, and that the same. Nor yet are the miracles which they maintain to have been done by means of their temples at all comparable to those which are done by the tombs of our martyrs. If they seem similar, their Gods have been defeated by our martyrs as Pharaoh's magi were by Moses" (*De Civ. Dei*, xxii. 10). St. Augustine goes on to explain that the martyrs are not worshipped as gods, for "they are not invoked by the sacrificing priest. It is to God, not to them, that he sacrifices."

desires of those who call upon them.

3. The "treasury of merits" is not, so far as I know, a doctrine which has developed. Merit, in this expression, stands not for merit in the strict sense, but for satisfaction. That in the time of St. Cyprian the martyrs were considered to make a greater satisfaction for their sins than was needed by themselves, is certain ; and it was believed that these satisfactions could be transferred to others, on account of the communion of saints, not indeed by the martyrs themselves, but by the ecclesiastical authority. The custom of shortening the time of canonical penance (commonly called indulgence) was at an early period based on the use of these satisfactions of the Saints. It does not appear that any evolution of the doctrine has taken place, only in practice the penance has fallen into desuetude, while the indulgences have been given more and more freely.[1]

4. The position of Mary as *Theotokos*, or Mother of God, is the highest that the Church ascribes to her, and the highest which can be ascribed to any mere creature. It is given to her in the Gospels, and the approval of the name in the Council of Ephesus hardly amounts to a development. But devotion in

[1] That is to say, *nominally* much larger indulgences are granted. But then, the signification of the measures (40 days, 3 years, "plenary," etc.) has changed. These no longer mean a definite relaxation on earth, but simply denote the *relative* values of the various indulgences in the intention of the Church. It is obvious that we have no means of knowing what degree of "loosing in heaven" corresponds to each degree of "loosing on earth." Nor can we tell how far an indulgence is actually gained. But we are certain that the Church has the power of loosing, though we cannot see its effects with our bodily eyes or feel them.

the course of ages has certainly understood the place of Mary better and better in her relation to us. If we become the children of God by incorporation into the body of her Son, we necessarily become her children at the same time; and the love of Mary, so highly developed already in some of the Fathers in the fourth century, has certainly become more filial, more tender, as well as more diffused. In earlier times the martyrs, then recent, were greater objects of devotion. As the Church realised that Mary is queen of the martyrs and of all the Saints, and far closer to Christ, and at the same time far more bound to us, than any of them can be, devotion to Mary grew and widened.[1] The Church cannot insist too much on the true position of Mary, for it is a strong hedge round the doctrine of the Incarnation. Every grace of Mary's, every prerogative, every dignity she has, is hers simply because she is the Mother of Christ; and it is wholly for His sake that we honour her, nor do we give her any honour which does not in consequence redound to Him of necessity.[2]

To these examples of developments, chosen by Dr. Gore himself,

we may add two more of greater importance, for they are the two which commonly cause the greatest difficulty to non-Catholics. I mean, of course, the infallibility of the Pope and the Immaculate Conception of Mary.

1. As to Papal Infallibility, see chapters vi. and vii.

2. The Immaculate Conception is a particularly interesting instance of development. Three Fathers of the second century — St. Justin Martyr, St. Irenæus, and Tertullian —call Mary the second Eve, as Christ was the second Adam.[3] They emphasise her co-operation (of course, in a wholly subordinate sense) in the work of the redemption of man as parallel to the part played by Eve in the fall. The obedience of the second Eve reversed the curse which had fallen on the first Eve by her disobedience. The same views are repeated in succeeding centuries. In the fourth century the absolute and perfect purity of Mary from all sin is constantly preached.[4] Epiphanius,

---

[1] Probably Dr. Gore thinks it has gone too far, and no doubt this may be true in this or that case; I do not know; at all events, no one is bound to copy or to admire Neapolitan flowers of piety, such as were necessary to the excitable people for whom St. Alphonsus wrote; nor is anyone forced to believe that Saint's well-known teaching that all graces are distributed by God through the hands of Mary. It is a harmless doctrine, but it is one not easy to prove theologically.

[2] Protestants have often said (I am not thinking of Dr. Gore) that we Catholics put our Lady in the place of Christ. I fear it is true that the place in which many Protestants put Christ is much the same as that in which we rightly put His Mother, that is to say, the highest place among creatures, but yet at an infinite distance from her Son and Creator.

[3] St. Justin, *Dial.* 100, p. 327 C.; St. Irenæus, *Hær.*, III. 22 and V. 19; Tertullian, *De Carne Christi,* 17.

[4] Dr. Gore's view is given on page 70: "Where an opinion has been commonly held by Churchmen, like the actual sinlessness of the blessed Virgin, but cannot plead quite universal consent nor the authority of Holy Scripture, it will rank rather as a pious opinion than as an article of faith." 'Quite universal' is a strong expression. Such a test would be too severe for most of the cardinal doctrines of the faith. But the difficulties in this case are almost nil. If St. Chrysostom seems to imply some weakness and ignorance in our Lady, it should not be forgotten, when he thus contradicts the general opinion, that he belongs to that literal school of exegesis which brought forth the impugners of the divine maternity of Mary, Theodore of Mopsuestia and Nestorius. It is greatly to St. Chrysostom's honour that the trace of contagion is so exceedingly slight. As for Scripture, the Fathers would not have admitted that its authority is lacking.

Ambrose, Ephrem may be cited as witnesses from the Greek, the Latin, and the Syrian Churches. St. Augustine has even been thought to say in two famous passages that she was free from original sin. However this may be, it was evidently impossible that this question should be asked when as yet the doctrine of original sin itself had not been fully elucidated. After St. Augustine's works against the Pelagians, this latter doctrine was much in view, and consequently the question whether our Blessed Lady contracted the sin of Adam or not was discussed. There was no difficulty about one point. It was soon everywhere taught that Mary was *born* in a state of grace. St. John Baptist was filled with the Holy Ghost in his mother's womb, and the Fathers taught that he was consequently born in grace, like a child who is baptised before its birth. The privilege for our Blessed Lady would therefore not be unique, and less than this could certainly not satisfy the sayings of the Fathers as to her freedom from all sin. But was even this sufficient? The affirmative reply was confined to a few theologians. Only its patronage by St. Bernard gave it prominence. At what precise point of time after her conception and before her birth must the cleansing from sin have taken place? No answer was forthcoming. The more obvious and natural view was expressed in the popularity of the Feast of the Conception. It was not hard to see that the only moment which could be imagined as suitable for the first influx of the Holy Spirit into Mary was the first moment of her existence in her mother's womb; for any subsequent moment there was nothing to be urged. Further, this explanation abundantly satisfied the belief of the Church in the exemption of the Mother of God

from all sin. But though the pious opinion spread among the people, it met with opposition from a few theologians, including St. Thomas Aquinas. In the first place, there was the authority of St. Bernard against it. Then it seemed a novelty; it was easy to reply that St. Bernard had not understood the doctrine, and that there was no novelty, but only the limitation of an old truth by a more precise definition of its import. An, at first sight, more serious objection was found : it was asked how it could be said that Mary was redeemed from sin, if sin never touched her at all? It was the glory of the *Doctor subtilis*, Duns Scotus (an Irishman, it is now said), to have given a reply which was found satisfactory to all ; the most perfect form of redemption is to be delivered from the devil in such a way that he has no opportunity at all of exercising his power. The precious Blood of Jesus Christ would have been foiled of an effect which it was capable of producing if none of the progeny of Adam had been saved from all effects of his sin. When this was seen to be reasonable, there was no longer any possibility of doubting the answer to the question originally proposed. At the same time the scriptural evidence became clearer. The woman who makes war against the dragon in the Apocalypse is mystically the Church, but literally she is the Mother of a Divine Child, so that she is Mary taken as a type of the Church. Thus the prophecy in Genesis is fulfilled, and the words of the early Fathers about the second Eve are justified.

This is a very bare outline of the development of the dogma. Dr. Gore will presumably say that he thinks it, after all, a novelty. He thereby places himself in the posi-

tion of those mediæval doctors who eventually got the worst of the argument. It is not an absurd position, for great men were found in it. But it has been considered for hundreds of years to have been disposed of and refuted. And further, if Dr. Gore rejects the doctrine, this is just as much a development or an innovation as if he accepted it. He can certainly find no anticipation of such a denial in antiquity. Suppose he should reply : " I do not deny the doctrine, neither do I accept it ; the question was left a mystery in early times, and it was intended by God to remain a mystery." I do not know that he would say this, but if he should do so, it would show that he had not comprehended the cause which necessitated the development. Two principles were in collision, both of them received by the Church from the Apostles. The one asserted that Mary was the second Eve, and in a sense co-redemptress of the human race, and wholly pure from all touch of sin, the vanquisher of the devil, and not his slave. The other asserted, though later, that St. Paul taught that all men had fallen under the curse of Adam. It was utterly impossible to leave the two dogmas in their apparent contradiction without attempting an explanation. It was just a case in which the Church would show that she was a mere human organisation if she could not interpret and harmonise her own teaching. She could not claim to be the "pillar and ground of the truth" if she could propose contradictory views for the faithful to believe. But she is not inspired ; and though the promised assistance of the Holy Spirit makes her infallible when at length she holds a truth unanimously, or defines it with authority, yet the preparation is ages long.

The opposition of the two doctrines has been done away with by Protestants by the simple expedient of dropping one of the two doctrines, and that the older of the two in patristic attestation. The Church of God cannot act thus ; she cannot omit or alter what she has received. And lo, when in the fifteenth century, or a little earlier, a unanimous result is reached, it is seen that both *the seemingly opposite doctrines have been confirmed and elucidated.* Original sin, indeed, claimed Mary as its subject, but she was preserved from it and from the power of the devil in such a unique way that she owes more to the merits of her Son than does the greatest of sinners and than any other creature whatever ; yet this very redemption consisted in her total exemption from that from which she was redeemed, and in the first instant of her conception she was utterly immaculate.

This example has been drawn out at some length because if it is well understood there is no need of other instances. We see how perfectly the demands of St. Vincent have been carried into effect. The two great doctrines involved have been explained ; a particular instance has been drawn forth from a general principle. Yet nothing whatever has been added, only the fulness of the meaning and application has been brought out, and the result is more plainly scriptural than were either of the premises. The Immaculate Conception has thus *always* been held, and *everywhere*, and *by all—semper et ubique et ab omnibus* — with the exception of those few professed theologians whose office under Providence it was to elucidate it while they opposed it. The present settlement of the question has been arrived at by consulting and harmonising the past. The Protestant world has, as usual, decided it by ignoring the Bible and the Fathers, and by inventing a new dogma of a sin-enslaved Mary, of which antiquity never heard.

B.

Dr. Gore imagines an Anglican to put forward the difficulty : How are we—not professed theologians or even students—to find out the "rule of faith"? " The Roman idea of Church authority gives a simpler remedy for our difficulties. Theirs is a rule of faith of easy access" (pp. 48, 49).

In reply, he distinguishes between a proximate and an ultimate rule of faith. The former " consists of the personal teachers to whom by God's providence we are subject," together with " the written formulas of the Church, . . . the creed and catechism, the offices and ceremonies."

No doubt, as Dr. Gore says, this " proximate rule of faith is of easy access." But is it a " rule" at all? The catechism, offices, and ceremonies of the Church of England have not the approbation of what Dr. Gore holds to be the rest of the true Church on earth. As for the personal teachers, as there is no general agreement in the Anglican communion, what they may happen to teach must depend principally upon chance. This easily accessible "rule" does not inspire one with much confidence in its guidance.

The "ultimate rule of authority or remoter rule of faith" involves " a comparison of records, a searching into the past traditions of the Church. Such research is only possible, comparatively, for a few, and only a few are capable of undertaking it." This is exceedingly distressing. · Are these few competent persons the only ones who

know the truth? "The few act for the many." Where do they publish their results? I know of many students of patristic literature and of the history of dogma in the present, and still more in the past; undoubtedly the majority are Catholics, but I should not have ventured to call any of them fully "competent" on so momentous a matter as the determination of the true faith. The most prominent of them all at the present day is Dr. Harnack, whose views on the earlier period of Church history Dr. Gore would reject even more entirely than I should. There is no consent to be found, if we are simply referred to scholars in general ; and instead of obtaining guidance, we shall be more puzzled than ever. St. Vincent of Lerins would certainly not have sent us to the scholars, but to the Church.[1]

[1] In a long note (pp. 50, 51) Dr. Gore gives from Mahan's *Exercise of Faith* an abstract of advice given by St. Chrysostom to a *heathen* seeking the truth. I will not criticise it in detail, but will quote the conclusion :—

" In this particular instance, St. Chrysostom, after asking the man whether he had not a mind and a judgment of his own, proceeds to give him such marks of the true Church as he could, and leaves him to make his way clear through the mazes of this complex guidance." This is just what any Catholic instructor would do. *Those who are outside* must use their own private judgment to find the truth. The way we show them (if they ask for guidance, and are already inclined to become Christians) is the way to the Catholic Church, and we explain to them her credentials. If once they submit to her claims, by the use of their reason and the gift of faith, they cannot exercise their private judgment any further with regard to those truths which she proposes for their acceptance. For evidently if they reject her authority on a single point they show their want of faith in her infallibility as a teacher as much as if they rejected all. The question before us in dealing with the authority of the Church is not with regard to unbelievers, but to those who are Christians already. We are

But again he urges: "The Fathers do not seem to shrink from recommending, even to ordinary inquirers, a difficult way of arriving at the truth" (p. 50). No one, I think, who knows anything of the Fathers will accept such a statement without limitation. The usual teaching of the Fathers is that we must simply accept the teaching of the Church throughout the world. There is no variety in their teaching on this point.

They are ready to "dry up all the rivulets of heretical propositions with nothing beyond the Sun of the Church," as St. Jerome's fine phrase has it.[1] But there are occasions when it is hard to discover what the Church does teach. These more easily occurred in early times than now—to mention one cause only, the means of communication were not what they are now—and in such exceptional cases it was occasionally necessary to supply some additional directions suited to the circumstances. Dr. Gore's first instance is unfortunate. "Tertullian witnessed in his day the spectacle of 'one and another—the most faithful, the wisest, the most experienced in the Church, going over to the wrong side'" (p. 51). Yes, and what is the remedy that he proposes (would that he had taken it himself) to counteract this evil? The ap-

peal, not to scripture, not to the wisdom of the teacher, but to "prescriptive right."

"Which was first in the field, the Gnostic, or the Church throughout the world?" The test was perfectly simple as well as perfectly conclusive. It may be applied just as well to-day as in the year 200—there is now, as then, but one historic Church to claim our allegiance. "If ever," says Dr. Gore, "a clear rule of faith, a papal voice, a centre to Christendom was needed, it was then." But the clear rule of faith was there. As for a centre of Christendom, Rome was even then the centre of communion, by the admission of all scholars; and to Rome, where the Apostles poured forth their faith together with their blood, Tertullian refers his readers, as to the nearest Church of Apostolic foundation; though all the Churches held the same faith and would give the same witness. But why "a papal voice" was wanted I cannot conceive.[2] The voice of the Church collective was perfectly certain and well known, and the heretics despised it. They would not have attended any better to the voice of the Church's head, speaking in her name. Besides, the heretical leaders had actually all gone to Rome in succession, in the hopes of gaining her to their side—Valentinus, Cerdo and Marcion, Apelles, Potitus, Basiliscus and Syneros, and the female foundress of the Carpocratians, Marcellina. All had come, and had been cast out, just as the Montanists and the Monarchians, within the next twenty years after Tertullian was writing, were to come thither and to be likewise cast out.

not inquiring how the great Mogul or the Empress of China should be converted, but how Dr. Gore comes to know the true form of the Christian religion so securely that he is able to publish a book in which, with some confidence (if not with unshaken certainty), he ventures to disagree with nearly all Christians. For I must never cease to harp upon this cardinal point, that I have with me (or rather I am on the side of) half the Christians of the world, while Dr. Gore has only a few (*i.e.* moderate High-Churchmen) who agree with him. Is he one of the "few," one of the "competent persons," who are able to tell us what the ancients really held?

[1] *Adv. Lucif.*, 28.

[2] A "papal voice" did address Tertullian, with a "peremptory edict" as if (he says ironically) from a bishop of bishops, a Pontifex Maximus. But he was then a heretic, and would not listen.

But a papal pronouncement *ex cathedra* is for the assurance of Catholics, rather than for the conversion of heretics; and I do not see why Dr. Gore thinks it would have been effective against the Gnostics!

"Once more, the years of the Arian controversy were years of deepest distress. Again a papal voice of authority was sorely needed, if ever. But in the moment of uttermost strain and profoundest peril the Pope did something very different from giving a clear voice for the guidance of Christians. He repudiated Athanasius, the great upholder of the truth, and left him 'alone against the world'" (pp. 51, 52).

If Liberius momentarily fell, he was firm both before and after. The weakness of Hosius and Liberius availed the Court party less than their persecution disgraced it. Dr. Gore is hard to please. When Athanasius found himself deprived of his see in 339 or 340, he himself appealed to the Pope. The Pope summoned him to Rome, and he obeyed.[1] The Eusebian party were also summoned, but they did not obey. Eventually the Pope, after awaiting them in vain, assembled a synod at Rome and acquitted Athanasius. If this was not a papal "voice of authority," I do not know what is. This decision was

[1] St. Julius says, quoted by Athanasius, *Apol.*, 29: "For he did not come of himself, but was summoned by letters from us, as we wrote to you." So Theodoret, *Hist. Eccl.*, ii. 3: "Athanasius, knowing their plot, retired and betook himself to the West. For to the bishop of Rome (Julius was then Shepherd of that Church) the Eusebians had sent the false accusations which they had put together against Athanasius. And he (Julius), *following the law of the Church*, both ordered them to repair to Rome, and also summoned the divine Athanasius to judgment. And he, for his part, started at once on receiving the call: but they who had made up the story did not go to Rome, knowing that it would be easy to see through their falsehood." Cp. Sozom., iii. 10; Athan., *Apol.*, 20; *Hist. Arian.*, 11.

always upheld by Julius, and by his successor Liberius, except apparently on one unfortunate occasion, after an exile borne on this account for two years, apart from all friends and advisers. Pope Julius restored Eastern bishops to their sees on his own authority.[2] Pope Liberius quashed the unorthodox decree into which the Council of Ariminum had been betrayed. The position of Rome during this period is best summed up in the words which St. Gregory Nazianzen wrote in his retirement later on, when the East was still unsettled after its long

[2] Socrates, ii. 15, says he did so on the ground that the Roman Church had primatial rights. Sozomen, iii. 8, "alleging that the guardianship of all belonged to him on account of the dignity of his see." Dr. Gore quotes the latter passage (p. 101, note), and actually thinks worth while to point out that it does not follow from the words of Sozomen that he admitted the plea of Pope Julius. True, but his general account of the deeds of Julius and Liberius proves sufficiently his opinion of their position. St. Athanasius, at all events, admitted the plea! But Dr. Gore is really astonishing when he goes on: "Mr. Rivington curiously enough has not gone on to quote Sozomen's account of how the Orientals dealt with his claim to authority." These Orientals are Eusebius of Nicomedia, the leader of the heretical Court party, and his Arianising friends! Really the late Dr. Rivington could hardly be expected to be so unfriendly to Dr. Gore as to anticipate that he would identify himself with such a crew! It was necessary for them to evade the papal authority, under which Athanasius and orthodoxy had a safe refuge. This is why they wrote a letter "full of insincerity" (εἰρωνείας), says Sozomen, who hates them with all his heart. Truly Dr. Gore strays into strange company. He adds, "Nor did Dr. Rivington mention that Sozomen's account of Julius's claim, as tested by his own letters, is exaggerated." True, once more; and there are other cases where we find both Socrates and Sozomen, fifth-century Greek historians, *making more of the papal prerogative* than the actual circumstances or words on which they comment need imply (see also ch. vi.). It was natural for them to see it where a modern will hesitate to make the inference.

troubles: "The faith of the one (Rome) was right long since and is so yet, binding the whole West with her saving word."[1] In the East, during the Arian troubles, it is true that there was great difficulty in finding out the truth. Heretics had got the power by intrigue, and kept it by lying. All claimed to have the old faith and to be in communion with Rome. But such times of stress and storm are exceptional. Dr. Gore seems inclined to regard them as normal and even desirable. "And indeed is not this difficulty, this requirement of patience in finding out the truth, part of the probation of faith? It is just what is suited to our time of discipline" (p. 52). But according to Dr. Gore, when we think we have found it (by digging in the early centuries), there is no living voice to tell us whether we are right or wrong.[2] It is well to seek, if we expect to find; but Dr. Gore's idea of seeking what we shall have

no means of recognising when we come across it, is simply a proposal to spend our life in puzzling over a riddle which has no answer.

Let us put the rival rules of Faith side by side. Dr. Gore says: Go and find out what the early Church believed. We say: Come and accept what the living Church teaches.

1. Dr. Gore's rule is illogical, for it begs the question: 'What reason have we for trusting to the first three centuries, or the first five?' The Church of those centuries does not tell us that the subsequent ages would go astray. This rule does not fulfil the Vincentian rule, "always, everywhere, and by all."[3]

[1] *Carmen de Vita Sua*, i. 562.

[2] But Dr. Gore says, "I must protest that the authority of the Church is, as we Anglicans understand it, a most real guidance of our spirit and intellect to which, by God's mercy, we love to submit ourselves." Is he sure that these words, which he evidently means so solemnly, are in correspondence with facts? Is it not possible that he is deceiving himself and others? For to an outsider it is so apparently obvious that Dr. Gore has not accepted a rule of faith from his own Church, nor from any other authority than himself. I do not for an instant doubt that Dr. Gore loves to submit, believes that he is submitting, and has the merit of submitting, but for none of his doctrines has he, in the last analysis, any other ground than his own opinion that they express the doctrine of the Church. He believes seriously that he is submitting to the Church, while he is after all submitting to himself.

With regard to a general council, Dr. Gore says, " With what infinite joy would we hail its possibility !" But this is somewhat discounted by the explanation on p. 42 that the "authority of general councils

only became decisive after their verdict had been accepted in the Church at large." This seems to mean that the Church of England would not be bound to accept the decision of a general council unless she *did* accept it. As a historical fact it may be well to remark in passing that Dr. Gore is mistaken. Except in the case of the first general council (as to which the evidence is defective) there is no doubt that it was the confirmation by the Pope which gave them binding force.

[3] With regard to this Vincentian canon itself a word is necessary. The test *quod semper, quod ubique, quod ab omnibus* is proposed by St. Vincent in cases where the present teaching of the Church has been impugned or seems to be doubtful. He does not put it forward as the ordinary rule of faith, but as a test for emergencies. Dr. Gore quotes Cardinal Manning as saying: "The appeal to antiquity (*i.e.* the appeal behind the present teaching of the Church) is both a treason and a heresy." The Cardinal is speaking of an appeal *against* the present teaching of the Church. There can be no doubt that St. Vincent of Lerins would have agreed.

One other point must also be mentioned, because Dr. Gore has failed to bring it out. St. Vincent does not think it necessary to understand by antiquity the very earliest times, but is content with the witness of the age preceding the raising of a new question; for consent in any one period is sufficient. This is because he held the Church to be infallible, so that consent at any one moment implied consent always.

For in the first place it frequently, in Dr. Gore's hands, gives results which are better described by "recently, in England, and by a few."

In the second place, Dr. Gore's rule itself has absolutely no claim to antiquity, universality, or consent.

Finally, it is impossible, for by its use no two persons will arrive at the same result.[1]

2. The Catholic principle is logical, for it carries out the idea (which Dr. Gore also holds) of a divinely founded and assisted Church to its legitimate result. It fulfils the Vincentian rule, for the whole Church has always taught everywhere the same doctrine. Instead of impossible, it is easy of access and plain —not a puzzle for the learned, but a help for the simple.

Dr. Gore holds a principle which must lead him right if he follows it out. For him, Church authority is not a present fact, but the historical witness of a dead Church of ages ago. But a careful scrutiny of those primitive ages, though it may leave many important doctrines uncertain, yet must necessarily throw into brilliant light the claim of the Church in those early days not merely to be then living, vocal, authoritative, infallible, but to possess these qualities as an unfailing endowment until the end of the world. If to St. Irenæus, to St. Athanasius, to St. Augustine (for instance) the voice of the Church of their day was without appeal, this was because the same unbroken unity, the same universality, with the same compelling voice, were to endure until Christ should come again.

CHAPTER IV

THE BIBLE IN THE CHURCH

IN this chapter I cannot see that there is much to quarrel about. Dr. Gore summarily rejects "the Bible and the Bible only" as the rule of faith. He tries indeed to make an antithesis between his position and the Catholic teaching. His rule of faith is "the Bible interpreted by the Church." The Council of Trent has declared that the Church "receives and venerates

---

[1] It is true that he says on p. 53 : "And practically a prayerful and patient Christian *can* find out the truth with quite sufficient security." In view of the present state of Anglican beliefs, is this ironical? Is it so *obvious* that Dr. Gore is more right than Prebendary Webb-Peploe, or Mr. Spencer Jones, or Mr. Beeby, or Canon Hensley Henson? or than Harnack or Duchesne?

with an equal feeling of piety and reverence all the books of the Old and New Testament . . . and also the traditions relating to faith and morals," etc. There is no obvious contradiction between these two rules. Dr. Gore accepts tradition as well as Scripture as his rule of faith. So does the Council of Trent. Modern theologians make a convenient division of traditions into three species : according as they (1) merely interpret plain words of Scripture, or (2) deduce from principles laid down in Scripture, or (3) add something which is not contained in Scripture. Of these three classes the first two are incomparably the most numerous and important.[1] Dr. Gore holds to their necessity and importance, and we therefore agree in the main point. The question is solely about the third kind.

1. In the first place Dr. Gore believes fully in the chief point which has to be proved by tradition alone. I refer of course to the inspired canon of Holy Scripture itself. The canon may indeed be partially defended by criticism, as Dr. Gore points out (p. 60), and the inspiration of the Old Testament (though not its canon) is witnessed to by the New. Yet Dr. Gore will not deny that it is from the Church that he gets his Bible, nay he asserts it.

2. But Dr. Gore actually holds, on the authority of tradition alone, a doctrine which the Catholic Church does not! The Bible certainly does not anywhere say that it contains the whole of Christian doctrine, and that nothing can be of faith which cannot be proved by its witness. Dr. Gore has naturally not attempted any proof of this dogma from Scripture, still less from reason. The only proof he vouchsafes is a patristic one. I cannot help thinking it somewhat illogical to prove by tradition alone that tradition alone is an insufficient proof in such matters.

3. What, on the other hand, do Catholic theologians teach? While they declare that there exist unwritten traditions in the Church which are not in the Bible, they simultaneously give from the Bible the proofs of every doctrine they discuss. If we ask for an example

of an unwritten tradition, they suggest the observance of Sunday and of Lent, or the baptism of infants. There is at all events not a single controverted doctrine (except that of the inspiration and the canon of Holy Scripture) for which they do not offer scriptural proof. Surely Dr. Gore's fear of unwritten traditions is a very bugbear. The few doctrines which Catholic theologians profess to have from tradition alone are practices (involving doctrine) to which Dr. Gore has no objection whatever.[2]

4. But he claims that the Fathers taught this sufficiency of Scripture. The three passages he has quoted, however, do not prove quite so much as he thinks. Origen, in the first place, is the prince of allegorists, and was capable of making Scripture mean absolutely anything. The passage from St. Vincent is incorrectly translated.[3] St. Athanasius speaks quite generally of the principal doctrines of Christianity. Many of the Fathers speak like this,

[1] It is not easy to put doctrines in one category or the other. I should myself put the Primacy of St. Peter and transubstantiation in the first class, as "declaratory" traditions. The full doctrine of the Holy Trinity seems to go into the second class, together with much of the doctrine of the sacraments.

[2] Perhaps the perpetual virginity of Mary is a doctrine which really rests upon tradition alone. The invocation of Saints is usually grounded on Scripture by theologians. Such practices as Dr. Gore might dislike are regarded as developments, not as traditions.

[3] On p. 65 Dr. Gore has rendered: "Here, perhaps, someone will ask, What need is there—seeing that the canon of the Scriptures is perfect, and in itself suffices to the full for all demands—that the authority of the ecclesiastical interpretation should be joined to it?" But St. Vincent really says, "and suffices to itself to the full for all its purposes" (*sibique ad omnia satis superque sufficiat*), *i.e.* in itself Scripture is not ambiguous, and needs no interpreter. Dr. Gore may press *ad omnia* if he wishes, but it is at best vague, and does not amount to an assertion that Scripture "suffices of itself to all demands." Again, on p. 66, there is the same mistranslation of "*non quia canon solus non sibi ad universa sufficiat,*" which appears as: "Not because the canonical Scripture is not *of itself* (!) sufficient for all things."

and we are all agreed that in fact all the main truths of our religion are to be found in the Bible.

5. There are conversely very numerous places in which the Fathers defend as Apostolic tradition what they cannot find in Holy Scripture.[1] Dr. Gore is evidently not unaware of this. "The Fathers," he says, "in general draw a distinction between the authority of Scripture for doctrine and the authority of unwritten tradition for practice. Cf. Tertul., *De corona*, 3, 4. St. Chrysostom on 2 Thess. ii. 15, and Epiphanius, *Hær.*, lxi. 6, should be interpreted in accordance with this principle." But the Fathers draw no such distinction.[2] It is

true that, as is shown in the footnote, the traditions which they give as instances are mainly practices

from the divine Scripture. Wherefore the holy Apostles handed down some things in writings, some things in tradition." This cannot be interpreted in accordance with Dr. Gore's proposed principle, for St. Epiphanius's instance is not a custom, but a doctrine: "The holy Apostles of God have handed down to the holy Church of God that it is a sin to turn to marriage, after having decided upon virginity." Whether we believe the statement or not, at least it is clear that St. Epiphanius is thinking of doctrines. Again, the same Father thus defends prayer for the dead (*Hær.*, lxxv. 9): "The Church does this of necessity, having received the tradition from the Fathers," etc. St. Epiphanius was unacquainted with Maccabees. If that book had been in his Bible, he would have placed this doctrine in the first class, among declarative traditions, as is done by modern theologians. I suppose Dr. Gore does not receive the book. Does he then find means to defend prayers for the dead out of the Protestant Bible? He certainly believes in their being an Apostolic tradition, but how about the proof from Scripture?

We next come to the passage of St. Chrysostom: "Hence it is plain that they (the Apostles) did not hand down all things by letter, but many things without writing. But both the latter and the former are equally to be believed. So that we hold the tradition of the Church to be believed. It is a tradition: ask no more." But Dr. Gore does ask more: he wants to know whether the tradition is a practice or a doctrine before he will consent to accept it!

Now it is St. Basil's turn. Dr. Gore quotes: "It is a manifest falling from the faith and an argument of arrogancy, either to reject any point of these things that are written, or to bring in any of these things that are not written." Here "bring in" means "insert." The addition of anything which limits or contradicts seems to be intended. As for the passage *De Spir. S.* xxvii. 66, St. Basil speaks in the most general terms of doctrines, but his instances are of practices. To one of these especially, I would call attention: the blessing of oil for confirmation and its use, "the unction itself." We may prefer to find references to this in Scripture, (*e.g.* 2 Cor. i. 21, Eph. i. 13, 1 John ii. 20, 27), but St. Basil is content simply with the authority of Apostolic tradition.

---

[1] Of the authors quoted by Dr. Gore, Origen more than once appeals to tradition for the practice of infant Baptism as proof sufficient without Scripture. St. Vincent of Lerins praises Pope Stephen for his appeal to tradition in favour of the validity of Baptism by heretics, against St. Cyprian's scriptural arguments. Both these practices involved doctrine, and St. Vincent regards the rebaptism of heretics as, in his day, heresy. Both examples are frequently referred to by St. Augustine. With regard to the former he says: "That which the universal Church holds, and which has not been instituted by councils, but always retained, is rightly believed to be of Apostolic tradition." So *De Genesi ad litt.*, X. 23 (39); cp. *Serm.* 294, 13 (14), 17*(17), *De pecc. mer. et rem.*, i. 20 (28), iii. 2 (2). Speaking of heretical Baptism, he says: "Even as many things which are not found in the letters of the Apostles, nor in the councils of their successors, are believed to have been handed down and approved by them." (*De Bapt. c. Don.*, ii. 7 (12), and the same again, *ibid.*, v. 23 (31)). He argues the point *De Unit. Eccl.*, 22 (63), and c. Cresc., i. 33 (39). St. Augustine nowhere limits such traditions to practices, excluding doctrine. Nay, he infers doctrine from Apostolic customs.

[2] The famous passage of Tertullian, *De cor. mil.*, 2, 4, gives a list of Apostolic traditions not grounded on Scripture. Of these, two involve doctrine—oblations for the dead and in honour of the martyrs. The words of St. Epiphanius are quite general (*Hær.*, lxi. 6): "Traditions must also be used, for all things cannot be taken

and not doctrines, but this is not quite always the case, and (what is most important) these practices are but doctrines in act, in many of the examples. The evident conclusion is that the Fathers appealed to Holy Scripture for all the principal doctrines, but that there were minor points, chiefly embodied in customs, which they defended by tradition alone. This is exactly the practice of modern theologians.

Thus I think Dr. Gore has been too positive in rejecting doctrinal non-scriptural traditions on patristic authority.

6. But we must go further. I do not think that I differ seriously from Dr. Gore's meaning, but his way of expressing it is by no means correct. " The patristic conception of the rule of faith finds it, as we have seen, (*a*) in the Bible, (*b*) in the witness of the general Church interpreting the Bible." This is putting a simple matter backwards, and it becomes an arbitrary and unreasonable statement instead of a piece of the plainest common sense. One does not see *à priori* why all Christian truth should be exclusively contained in the Bible. It is a collection of writings which from a rationalist point of view is a scratch collection. We find three forms of an early gospel, a later gospel, a short piece of history, a number of letters, and a vision, the whole prefaced by the sacred books of the Jews. " Bible " is a misnomer, for *Biblia* in Greek and in Latin is a plural word. Catholic writers more frequently therefore use the equivalent but clearer expression, "holy Scripture." It is not a book by a single writer, like the Koran, and it looks *prima facie* so unlikely to be intended as a corpus of Christian doctrine that I cannot conceive how one could approach the modern student with

such a startling dogma in any hopes of its finding acceptance. Again, it would be indeed strange if Christ had founded a Church for the purpose of interpreting the Bible. One would have anticipated for the Church some more independent office. Yet when writing a chapter on the subject of the authority of the Church, this is the only office which Dr. Gore assigns to that authority.

Now the Fathers agree with modern Catholic theologians (that is to say, the latter agree with the former) in putting tradition first and the Bible second. Dr. Gore will of course remember the commencement of St. Irenæus's third book against heresies, in which that Father tells how the Apostles went throughout the world teaching what they had heard from Christ, and how we have still in writing what some of them preached : Matthew, Peter, Paul, and John. He goes on in the third chapter to point out that the Churches throughout the world bear consentient testimony to the Apostles' teaching, which they had received from the Apostles themselves or from their disciples. This is the idea of tradition in the earliest Fathers—the truths handed down from generation to generation, and attested by the Apostolical succession, which does not mean (as people seem to think) the succession of bishops from their consecrators, but that of bishops in the same see without a break. The Bible contains these same truths written down by Apostles or Apostolic men, but it is not their primary legacy to the Churches which they founded. It is secondary, though of higher dignity than the tradition of individual Churches, and equal in dignity to that of the whole Church. It becomes a test for tradition, and a divinely ordained means by which the Church's traditional teaching can possess that infallibility which was promised by her Founder.

It is evident, therefore, that the primary office of the Church is not to interpret the Bible, but to teach. What she teaches is what she has always taught, what the Apostles first taught her. She proves her teaching and illustrates it from the Bible. She shows that its teaching is in harmony with her own; and this harmony witnesses to the reality of her infallibility, and at the same time to the reality of the Bible's inspiration. It is now evident why she alone is its interpreter: it is because she knew its doctrines before they were committed to writing: the Gospels were written for her, the Epistles were addressed to her. She interprets them by her tradition, not by some special gift of inspiration, as some might understand Dr. Gore's theory to suppose.

When we have thus reversed the order of that theory, we understand at once the relation of the contents of the Bible to the contents of tradition. The Bible is a comprehensive collection. It is *à priori* unlikely that there should be any important doctrine which is not taught or mentioned or presupposed or referred to in it. On the other hand, it is to be expected that some minor points may by chance have met with no mention. Doctrines of less moment are usually to be deduced from or developed out of larger principles; consequently very few doctrines are found to be devoid of all support from Holy Scripture. Practices and customs, however, are less to be expected in such documents. This is what the Fathers have found, and modern theologians have followed suit.

But the most important point of all is this: The proofs of traditional doctrines given by the Fathers are sometimes inconclusive to the modern mind. The same is also true of the proofs offered by theologians, ancient, mediæval, and modern, from Holy Writ. The critic of to-day is not satisfied with a "text," but asks for the context, the intention of the writer, his habits and his period. Many old-fashioned proofs from the Old Testatment, when thus handled, tend to disappear. And in the New Testament it is also true that such rigorous methods, even where there is perfect fairness, make many points but vague and uncertain, if we have Holy Scripture alone to go upon. Dr. Gore will say that we have the Church to interpret for us. Yes; but that is only possible when she has a plain statement before her. The modern mind will no longer consider arguments from allusions to be interpretations. If we start with tradition, the slightest allusion or hint in favour of tradition is of immense value and has a real impressiveness; but if we start with the Bible as the "ultimate record of the faith" of which "the Church is the interpreter" (p. 62), though this may not look a totally different method, yet it lands us in the dilemma of either offering ill-grounded interpretations to a critical world, or of reducing our dogmas to a far smaller and vaguer set of propositions than Dr. Gore would desire.

I deny, therefore, that the Fathers considered "that Scripture is the sole source of revealed truth" (p. 69). It is the secondary source, and the Catholic Church has equal reverence for both sources.

But, in conclusion, I wish to repeat that I believe Dr. Gore is not very far from this view, and if once we agreed in believing in a visible Church, on this point the difference would be seen to lie more in words that Dr. Gore does not really mean, or which express his meaning imperfectly, than in the meaning itself.[1]

CHAPTER V

THE PROMISE TO ST. PETER

DR. GORE'S appeal is to Holy Scripture and the early Church. How he has been able to pen, and again and again to republish, the statements he makes in this chapter on St. Peter, I am at a loss to understand. The Bible and the Fathers teach quite plainly the primacy of St. Peter.

The most casual reader of Scripture must notice how incomparably more often St. Peter is mentioned in the Gospels than is any other of the disciples. Everyone must remark his eager and impulsive character. He seems to be always putting himself forward. It is Peter who asks leave to walk on the water.[2] It is Peter who takes our Lord and rebukes Him, when he hears the prophecy of the Passion.[3] It is Peter who cries out at a miracle, "Depart from me, for I am a sinful man, O Lord."[4] It is Peter who exclaims, "Thou shalt never wash my feet," and then, changed in an instant, urges a contrary prayer.[5] It is Peter who vehemently proclaims, "Though all should be offended, yet will not I,"[6] and who

asks, "Why cannot I follow Thee now?"[7] and it is Peter who takes one of the two swords, and makes a clumsy dash at the high priest's servant,[8] and who, in spite of the danger, follows His Master "afar off" to the palace of the high priest.[9] It is Peter who in his excitement thrice denies his Master with cursing and swearing.

The same eagerness makes him the spokesman of the Apostles. Peter asks our Lord to explain a parable.[10] Peter asks how often one must forgive a brother.[11] Peter calls attention to the dead fig tree.[12] Peter says, "Lord, sayest Thou this to us, or also to all?"[13] Peter says, "Behold, we have left all and have followed Thee. What shall we have for this?"[14] Peter says, "Lord, to whom shall we go? Thou hast the words of eternal life."[15] Peter, answering a question addressed to all, cries, "Thou art the Christ, the Son of the living God!"[16]

But is it only his natural vivacity which makes him the spokesman of the Apostles? Is it not also his position among the Apostles? To begin with, he is one of the three who are chosen above the twelve, who are mentioned first in the lists

[1] The first paragraph of this fourth chapter of Dr. Gore's is excellent, and contains in embryo what I have just been urging. It is a pity he spoilt it by the topsy-turvy doctrine which follows.

[2] Mt. xiv. 28.

[3] Mt. xvi. 22; Mc. viii. 32.

[4] Lc. v. 8.   [5] Jo. xiii. 9.

[6] Mt. xxvi. 33, 35; Mc. xiv. 29; Lc. xxii. 34.

[7] Jo. xiii. 37.   [8] Jo. xviii. 10.

[9] Mt. xxvi. 58; Mc. xiv. 54; Lc. xxii. 54; Jo. xviii. 15.

[10] Mt. xv. 15.   [11] Mt. xviii. 21.

[12] Mc. xi. 21.   [13] Lc. xii. 41.

[14] Mt. xix. 27; Mc. x. 28; Lc. xviii. 28.

[15] Jo. vi. 69.   [16] Mt. xvi. 16.

of the Apostles.[1] These three speak to our Lord apart, that He may tell them what He might have left unsaid in the presence of the rest.[2] He chooses them to be the witnesses of the raising of the dead,[3] of His Transfiguration,[4] and of His Agony.[5]   But even among these three it is Peter who is the spokesman.   He proposes to remain on Tabor: "It is good for us to be here."   And our Lord Himself recognises this leadership. "He saith to Peter: Could ye not watch?" He speaks as to the leader of the three. "He saith to Simon, Sleepest thou? Watch ye and pray."

In the same vein the evangelist speaks of the three as "Peter and they that were with him,"[6] and the same expression stands for the disciples in Luke viii. 45.   After the Resurrection, the Angel bids the women, "Go tell His disciples and Peter"[7]; and we find the same distinction of Peter from the rest in the Acts: "Peter with the eleven"; "Peter and the Apostles."[8] So also in St. Paul's account of the witnesses of the resurrection: "He was seen by Cephas, then by the twelve."[9]

Even in the incident of the tribute money the Fathers find an instance of Peter's headship. The collectors came to Peter for information, says St. Chrysostom, "because he seemed to be the first of the disciples"; and he follows Origen in tracing the question which arose among the disciples "at that hour," who was greatest in the kingdom, to their jealousy of the honour done to Peter by our Lord in paying the tribute for him by a miracle.[10]

As Peter is thus recognised as the spokesman of the disciples, so he is invariably mentioned first when joined with others.   There are about five-and-twenty places in the Gospels and the Acts[11] where the name of Peter occurs with other names, and in every single case the name of Peter stands first.

St. Paul gives the order: "Paul, Apollos, Cephas, Christ." He intends it, St. Chrysostom tells us, for an order of ascending dignity. The same occurs once more: "Whether Paul, or Apollos, or Cephas"; but further on we find a climax yet more remarkable: "The other Apostles, and the brethren of the Lord, and Cephas." "He puts the Coryphæus last," again observes St. Chrysostom; and even Father Puller allows that "it is fair to quote this passage in favour of St. Peter's primacy of order."[12]

There is *only one* place in Holy Scripture where St. Peter is not named first in rank: "James and Cephas and John, who are accounted pillars, gave to me and to Barnabas the right hand of fellowship" (Gal. ii. 9). Against the cardinal doctrines of Christianity objections may be made from isolated passages, in spite of other conclusive proofs. But the few passages have to be interpreted in accordance with the many.   Here we have a single instance against more than two dozen which are clear: thus the

---

[1] Mc. iii. 16; Lc. vi. 14; Acts i. 13; Andrew, however, is put next to Peter by Mt. x. 2, as his brother.
[2] Mc. xiii. 3.
[3] Mc. v. 37; Lc. viii. 51.
[4] Mt. xvii. 1; Mc. ix. 2; Lc. ix. 28.
[5] Mt. xxvi. 37; Mc. xiv. 33.
[6] Lc. ix. 32.   [7] Mc. xvi. 7.
[8] Acts ii. 14 and v. 29.   Cp. Ignat. *Smyrn.* iii. 2.   [9] 1 Cor. xv. 5.

[10] Matt. xvii. 23; Origen *in Matt.* xiii. 14; Chrys. *in Matt. hom.* 58 (59), 2.
[11] Dr. Gore (p. 83) points to Acts viii. 14 as a proof that St. Peter was not Primate; "The Apostles sent Peter and John." That is, Peter and his colleagues sent Peter and John.   How on earth is this to be made to contradict St. Peter's supremacy?
[12] 1 Cor. i. 12; iii. 22; ix. 5. Chrys. *in* 1 *Cor. hom.* 3 and *hom.* 21 (vol. x. p. 24, 172). Puller, *Primitive Saints*, 3rd ed. p. 111.

Protestant argument from this passage that St. Paul did not admit any primacy in St. Peter falls to the ground.[1]

But St. Peter is not only mentioned first, he is actually called "the first," ὁ πρῶτος, in St. Matthew's list of Apostles (x. 2).

In consequence he is often called "first" by the Fathers, and they constantly mention his firstness or "primacy." Continually they repeat that he is "the first of the disciples," "the first in the Church," "the first of the Apostles,"[2] "the powerful and great one of the Apostles, on account of his virtue, their leader,"[3] "the most honoured,"[4] "the chosen, the elect, the first."[5] "Who should be unaware that St. Peter is the first of the Apostles?" asks St. Augustine,[6] as if addressing modern Protestants. Peter is "the tongue of the disciples, the voice of the heralds, the eye of the Apostles, the Keeper of heaven, the firstborn of those who bear the keys."[7] He is the leader or "coryphæus,"[8] an expression which is also applied to Peter, James, and John in the plural, or to Peter and Paul; but Peter is the κορυφαιότατος.[9] Similarly the Latins call him the Prince of the Apostles,[10] which in the singular only means St. Peter, though "the Princes of the Apostles" means Peter and Paul. The Fathers continually mention his primacy, *primatus*, *principatus*, and these expressions lead us on to the stronger titles. For *princeps*, from the time of Augustus onwards, had come to mean a ruler, a sovereign, though still capable of bearing its original meaning of simple firstness. There can be no doubt that St. Leo meant "ruler of the whole Church" when he said of Peter, "totius ecclesiæ princeps"; and his contemporary, St. Peter Chrysologus, the great bishop of Ravenna and Doctor of the Church, meant no less by the words, "Let Peter hold his ancient principality of the apostolic choir." Can we help similarly understanding St. Optatus's "Peter, that is, our prince"? or the "prince of the episcopal circle" of the Emperor Valentinian III."?[11] In St. Augustine's writings the word *princeps* frequently means ruler or emperor; are we to understand it in a milder sense whenever he applies it to St. Peter?[12]

But other titles have a clearer signification. The head of the Apostles [13] (a very common expres-

---

[1] There was some reason for this order. Probably James was the first of the three seen by St. Paul, and John the last. What is most noticeable is that to the Fathers this order of names was so unnatural that Irenæus, Tertullian, Gregory of Nyssa, Jerome, Ambrose, Augustine, are found to quote St. Paul as saying "Peter and James and John"! This reading is also found in the uncial MSS. D, E, F, G.

[2] For "first" no references need be given, as the expression is so universally applied to St. Peter. "First in the Church" (Chrys., *De Eleem.*, iii. 4.)

[3] Euseb., *Hist. Eccl.*, ii. 14. So Asterius, *Hom. in App. P. et P.*: "First Disciple, and greater among the brethren."

[4] Τιμιώτερος (Origen) Τιμιώτατος (Chrys.) προτιμώτερος (Asterius).

[5] Clem. Al, *Quis dives*, 21.

[6] *Tract* 56 *in Joann.*

[7] Ephrem Syrus, *Gr. in SS. App.*

[8] So, *e.g.*, Peter Alex., Athanasius, Cyril Hier., Macarius Ægyp., Eusebius, Epiphanius, Basil Seleuc., Isidore Pelus., Cyril Alex., Chrysostom, Proclus, Nilus, Theodoret, John Damasc., etc.

[9] Cyril Jerus. *Cat.*, ii. 15. Epiph., *Hær.*, 59.

[10] So, *e.g.*, Hilary, Optatus, Pacian, Jerome, Salvian, Sedulius, Augustine, Cassian, Leo, etc.

[11] Leo, *Serm.*, iv. 4. Peter Chrysol., Serm. 154. Optatus, ii. 4. Valentinian III., *apud Leon. Ep.* xi.

[12] St. Augustine often uses *princeps* of the Emperors, as other writers do, both secular and ecclesiastical. He found it in his Latin Bible in the sense of sovereign, *e.g.* "princeps huius mundi" (John xiv. 30), "principes huius sæculi" (1 Cor. ii. 6).

[13] *e.g.* Optatus, Jerome, Maximus Taur., Ephrem, Aphraates, Chrysostom, etc., etc.

sion) has surely more than a primacy of honour over the members. The Greek Fathers use the names "leader" (προστάτης, πρωτοστάτης, ἡγούμενος), "ruler" (ἄρχος, ἄρχηγος, ἔξαρχος), "the prominent one" (προέχων, προεκκείμενος). Most of these words postulate something more than rank. Father Puller has said that St. Peter had among the Apostles only the rank which the Duke of Norfolk enjoys among English peers. Is the Duke their πρωτοστάτης? Perhaps. But can he be considered their προστάτης, ἡγούμενος, or is not this the Lord Chancellor or the leader of the House? or is he their ἄρχος, ἔξαρχος,[1] or is not this the King? Suppose that any individual one of these expressions can be explained away, there yet remains their number, their frequency, their variety. It is not conceivable that the Fathers should have harped so consistently, persistently, insistently, on a supremacy which, in Dr. Gore's phrase, does not "carry with it any prerogative of primary importance." It is not necessary to dwell on this. The inference is sufficiently obvious.[2]

But it is a light thing that Peter should appear in the Bible as the mouthpiece of the Apostles and the first among them, and that he should invariably be mentioned in the place of honour. It is actually related there how our Lord promised him the primacy over the Church and how he invested him with it.

I. THE PRIMACY PROMISED
(Matt. xvi. 18–19)

"Thou art Peter; and upon this rock I will build My Church, and the gates of hell shall not prevail against it. And I will give to thee the keys of the kingdom of heaven. And whatsoever thou shalt bind on earth shall be bound in heaven, and whatsoever thou shalt loose on earth, it shall be loosed also in heaven."

Dr. Gore's explanation of this famous promise is as follows :—

"It is difficult, I think, to feel any doubt that our Lord is pronouncing the person of Peter to be the Rock. The Church as a human society is to be built on human characters, and in virtue of St. Peter's courageous act of faith in Himself, his deliberate acceptance of His Divine claim, our Lord sees in him, what He had hitherto failed to find among men, a solid basis on which His spiritual fabric may be reared, or at least a basis capable of

[1] Προστάτης (Basil Seleuc., Chrys.), προστασία (Chrys.), πρωτοστάτης (Proclus, Cyril Hier.), ἡγούμενος (Cyril Alex.), μέγιστος (Asterius), præcipuus (Maximus Taur.), ἄρχος (Greg. Naz.), ἄρχηγος (Epiphanius), ἔξαρχος (Acts of Council of Chalcedon, in speech of Philip, papal legate), προέχων (Cyril Alex.), προεκκείμενος (Cyril Alex.), πρόκριτος (Peter Alex., Cyril Alex.), προκριθείς (Greg. Naz., Basil), προκεκριμένος (Eusebius), προήγορος (Eusebius).

[2] Chrysostom, for instance, is fond of passages like these : "Peter, that head of the Apostles, the first in the Church, the friend of Christ, who received the revelation not from man but from the Father . . . this Peter, and when I say Peter, I mean the unbroken Rock, the unshaken foundation, the great Apostle, the first of the disciples, the first called, the first to obey"; "Peter, the coryphæus of the choir of the Apostles, the mouth of the disciples, the foundation of the Faith, the base of the confession, the fisherman of

the world"; "the first of the Apostles, the foundation of the Church, the coryphæus of the choir of the Apostles"; "the foundation of the Church, the vehement lover of Christ . . . he who ran throughout the world, who fished the whole world"; "this holy coryphæus of the blessed choir, the lover of Christ, the ardent disciple, who was entrusted with the keys of heaven, who received the spiritual revelation"; "Peter, the coryphæus of the choir, the mouth of all the Apostles, the head of that company, the ruler of the whole world, the foundation of the Church, the fervent lover of Christ." These passages are from *De Eleemos.* iii. 4 ; *Hom. de decem mille tal.* 3 ; *ad eos qui scandal. sunt* 17 ; *in illud. Vidi Dmn.* iv. 3 ; *In Act. App.* vi. 1 ; *in illud. Scitote quod in noviss. dieb.* 4.

being solidified by discipline and experience, till it become a foundation of rock on which the Church can rest" (p. 76).

The ancients would have said simply that the Church is built on men rather than have dragged in the abstraction "human characters." The rest of the sentence is good, though somewhat obvious.

Of the second part of the promise Dr. Gore says, "He goes on beyond all question to promise to invest him with an office, the office of steward in the Divine kingdom, with a supernatural legislative authority." So far, so good.

But Dr. Gore holds that St. Peter was not alone in his stewardship, or even as foundation, but that he merely shared these prerogatives, share and share alike, with the other Apostles. The solemn promise, with its impressive introduction— "Blessed art thou, Simon, son of Jona"—and with all the startling emphasis of its wording, though pronounced as the reward of Peter's bold confession, was not really a promise, was not really a reward to Peter in particular. It was a mere pretence of special favour, a deception, for the twelve were long since chosen, and they were all to receive exactly the same position which is here promised, as if it were a unique privilege, to one only. This is the plain meaning of Dr. Gore's interpretation, baldly put. I do not wish to characterise it, nor need I.

Over against this Dr. Gore puts forward as the "Roman" view what he calls the "mediatorial" position of St. Peter. He finds it in St. Leo the Great (surely one of the most eminent of primitive saints) and in St. Francis de Sales. He notes that Father Richardson repudiated the doctrine, while the late Dr. Rivington accepted it :—

"He is to be the Vicar of Christ upon earth. To him alone is primarily given the pastorate of souls and the authority of the keys. To the other Apostles these are only given mediately through him. Whatever they have, they have not directly from Christ, but indirectly from Christ through Peter."

It is quite easy for Dr. Gore to refute this dogma by merely pointing to the fact that in reality our Lord actually gave the power to forgive sins and the mandate to preach and to baptise to all the Apostles directly, and not through Peter. What stupid people these Romanists must be—Leo, Francis of Sales, Rivington—never to have noticed this plain fact; but then, of course, Romanists do not read their Bible ! Only I remember that a few pages back Dr. Gore was citing St. Leo as a witness to the necessity of Bible - reading, and Dr. Rivington was so long a Protestant that he can hardly have been forgetful of such important passages of Holy Scripture. Does not this, perhaps, suggest to Dr. Gore that there is a hitch somewhere ? Why not recognise that St. Leo means, and that St. Francis says, that our Lord Himself directly gave to His Apostles powers which were to be used in subordination to one among them, whom He constituted their head. This is all that is really meant by the imaginary "mediatorial position of St. Peter." The "gifts" which St. Leo says flow down to the whole body from Peter are the gifts which can only be given in subordination to his jurisdiction. The metaphor is not to be pressed until it becomes ridiculous, but as it is intended it is perfectly true, for less than this would not give any headship to St. Peter at all. For instance, in the diocese in which I live the jurisdiction all flows from the bishop, and since all the teaching, all the sacrifices, all the sacraments are administered by his direction, and cannot licitly be administered without it, it may rightly be said that the gifts of God flow to his flock only through him. But this does not imply that he must himself have *ordained* all the clergy of his diocese! The "mediatorial position of St. Peter" is not an expression familiar to Catholic theology, but if it is to be used, it must mean neither more nor less than I have said.

Dr. Gore admits that St. Peter had a kind of primacy, "which had to do with the opening of Church history" (p. 83).[1] In a note he adds, "This is Tertullian's view (*de Pudicitia*, c. xxi.), but his very powerful exposition is reduced in authority by the Montanist *animus* of the passage, which is aimed against the perpetuity of the power of 'loosing' in the Church." Tertullian is trying to show that the whole promise to St. Peter was personal to himself, and could not be used by the Church as deriving it from him. This treatise is about his latest and most spiteful, written when he had been some twenty years outside the Church. In this "powerful exposition" he is refuting the view taught by the Church he had deserted. This fact may well be said to "reduce" his authority! I am sincerely glad that, as a fact, the passage does not support Dr. Gore, whose view is diametrically

the opposite of Tertullian's (and far less objectionable), for he holds that the promises to St. Peter were meant for all the Apostles.[2]

Tertullian is apparently replying in the passage to a decree of Pope Callistus (c. 218-23), in which the "mediatorial" view (to use Dr. Gore's expression) was upheld. About 208, when only some eight years a heretic, Tertullian had taught that very doctrine, writing not against the Church, but against the Gnostics. "The Lord left the keys of the Church to Peter, and *through him* to the Church" (*Scorp.* 10). We can trace the same doctrine onwards in Africa. We shall presently see St. Cyprian deriving the authority of the bishop from St. Peter. St. Optatus in the fourth century is most explicit: "For the good of unity Blessed Peter deserved to be preferred before the rest, and *alone* received the keys of the Kingdom of Heaven, *that he might communicate them to the rest*" (i. 10). In St. Augustine the same idea occurs frequently; the keys, he says, were given to Peter as bearing the figure of the Church, and more than once he explains that it is because of his primacy that he thus represented the Church.[3]

---

[1] This primacy of action, held also by Lightfoot, is right as far as it goes. I am very glad Dr. Gore does not support the blasphemous idea preconised by Father Puller, that St. Peter had a primacy of honour only. Our Lord frequently told His Apostles that the first place among them was to be one of service to the rest; and can we dare to say that He Himself conferred upon St. Peter an empty honour?

[2] If it is astonishing that Dr. Gore should not have seen that Tertullian is directly opposed to him, it is not less so that this "powerful exposition" finds St. Peter's power of binding and loosing to have been principally exercised at the Council of Jerusalem, whereas Dr. Gore says, "He occupies no governing position in the Council of Jerusalem . . . the formal authority, the formal 'I decide,' comes from St. James." Tertullian has, of course, seen that Peter speaks last, after the discussion is over (Acts xv. 7), as St. Chrysostom points out: "He first permits the question to be moved in the Church, and then speaks" (on Acts *in loco.*; Oxf. trans. pp. 446, 447).

[3] I repeat the following references from an elaborate footnote on the subject in the

We must now turn to the text of St. Matthew itself. There are four different interpretations in the Fathers of the "rock."

(a) The ante-Nicene Fathers and the mass of later writers make St. Peter himself the rock. This Dr. Gore holds to be right, and so do I.

(b) After the rise of Arianism, the Fathers wished to emphasise St. Peter's declaration, "Thou art the Christ, the Son of the living God." Therefore they say sometimes that the Church is built on Peter's act of faith, his assertion ;

(c) Or they go further, and say it is built on the doctrine which he confessed.

(d) St. Augustine invented a new exegesis—that the rock is Christ.

The last opinion may be at once pronounced impossible. It rests on a distinction between *Petra* and *Petrus* which could not have been made in the language which our Lord was using ;[1] it would be hardly comprehensible unless our Lord said, "*but* upon this rock," instead of "*and* upon this rock"; and if St. Matthew had meant us to understand him thus, he would have told us that Christ pointed to

Revue Bénéd, Jan., 1903, pp. 37, 38, directed against the misunderstandings of Father Puller : "To Peter bearing the figure of the Church" (*de agone* 30 ; *Serm.* 149 6 ; 4 18 ; *Retract.* i. 21 ; *Tract* 118 *in Joann.*). "Almost everywhere Peter merited to bear the person of the whole Church" (*Serm.* 295 2 ; 75 9) etc., "on account of the primacy which he had among the disciples" (*Enarr. in Ps.* 108 1), "the first and chief in the order of the Apostles, in whom the Church was figured" (*Serm.* 76 3). "To Peter first, because among the Apostles Peter is first" (*Serm.* 295 4), etc.

[1] St. Augustine invented this interpretation as a part of his argument against the Donatists that the validity of the sacraments does not depend on the sanctity of the minister, because Christ acts in the minister. Peter has his name from Christ, *Petrus a Petra.*

himself as He spoke. St. Augustine himself does not venture to reject the usual interpretation, in favour of which he quotes a hymn of St. Ambrose, but he says the reader may choose. But now comes the important point. St. Augustine treats of the matter in his *Retractations*, a book in which he makes the most minute corrections in his former writings, all of which he passes under review. He tells us here that he has several times himself spoken of St. Peter as the Rock. He has done so in the following well-known passage of his acrostic hymn against the Donatists, which is a sort of popular ditty meant to be learnt by heart and sung by the people as an antidote to the Donatist claims :—

" Number the bishops from the see of Peter itself.
And in that order of Fathers see who succeeded whom,
That is the rock against which the gates of hell do not prevail."

(*Ps. c. partes Don.* str. 18).

We cannot doubt that St. Augustine would have been at great pains to remedy in such a composition the slightest point of doctrine which seemed to him to be ill-founded or ever so little misleading. He says in the *Retractations* that he is now inclined to think another explanation of the text more correct; but the doctrine founded on it (which is of course an infinitely more important matter) he leaves untouched. He had not ceased to believe that the Roman See, to the enumeration of whose bishops he so frequently appeals, was truly the rock upon which the Church is founded, and against which the gates of hell do not prevail. He had originally meant to emphasise in a telling way the position of that Church with which the Donatists were not in communion; and the remembrance of St. Peter the rock naturally suggested a transference (occasionally but rarely met with elsewhere among ancients and moderns) of the metaphor to Peter's see. Never does he suggest that though the metaphor might be mistaken, the fact expressed by it was doubtful. It is thus clear that the unusual interpretation of the rock by so thoroughgoing a Papalist as St. Augustine has no doctrinal significance whatever. Among the few writers who have followed St. Augustine the venerable Bede is chief. No one, I suppose, will suggest that St. Bede did not attribute a primacy of jurisdiction to St. Peter and his successors.

The third view, that the rock is the doctrine enunciated by Peter, is not a literal interpretation of our Lord's words. He cannot have meant: "Thou art Peter, and upon this fact that I am the Christ I will build My Church"; nor can it be shown that any ancient writer seriously proposed so unnatural an exegesis. Statements that the Church is built on the belief in our Lord's Divinity are *extensions* of the interpretation, just as St. Augustine mystically extended to Rome what was said of St. Peter.

The second interpretation may be thus expressed: "Thou art Peter, and upon thy firm faith in My Divinity I will build My Church." But in such a case there is no distinction between a man and his act. "Upon thy firm faith" is the same as "upon thee, for the firmness of thy faith." Thus the first and second views are practically identical, and the third is only an extension of the second. The three may be paraphrased thus:

1. Thou art Peter, a rock in confessing My Divinity, and upon thee I will build My Church.

2. Thou art Peter, and upon the rock of thy faith shown in confessing My Divinity I will build My Church.

3. Thou art Peter, and upon faith in My Divinity I will build my Church, in that I shall build it on thee.

The Fathers who give the second sense give it as an extension of the first; they do not mean it as the only possible one: hence we are not surprised to find both used by one and the same Father according to his needs. Similarly, the third is an extension of the second, and whoever uses it means to presuppose the second and the first also. Again we find these also used indifferently by the same writers, for instance, by Chrysostom and Epiphanius in the East, or by Hilary and Ambrose in the West.

We conclude of necessity, therefore, that the divergences of the Fathers in using this text are "significant," not of their carelessness about it, as Bishop Gore supposes, but of their sense of its importance. If we put aside St. Augustine's ingenious invention, it may fairly be said that the Fathers are unanimous in agreeing with Dr. Gore that St. Peter is the rock.[1] The confession which drew from our Lord such praise and such a dignity is set up, in consequence, by the Fathers as a sure antidote to heresy. It is because they recognise that for his confession St. Peter was made the rock-foundation of the Church that

[1] Ante-Nicene Fathers: Tertullian (thrice), Cyprian (often), Origen (often), Firmilian and Pope Stephen (in the letter of the former), Ps. Clementines, Treatise *de Aleatoribus* (this may be post-Nicene). Of post-Nicene Fathers I mention a few of the most eminent only: Eusebius, Hilary, Gregory Nyssen, Basil, Gregory Nazianzen, Pacian, Epiphanius, Ambrose, Jerome, Chrysostom, Cyril of Alexandria, and so on. In Syriac, Aphraates, Ephrem.

they infer the doctrine he confessed to be the foundation of Christian doctrine.

The second part of the promise needs little comment. Dr. Gore admits that Peter is made a steward of the kingdom, like Eliacim, the son of Helcias, in Isaias xxii. 22. But the essence of the office of steward is that it should be held by one man. I do not think the Fathers always realised that the possession of the keys meant this office of steward. But they often advert to the fact that only Peter receives the keys.[1]

One of the oldest commentators on this passage, and perhaps the most complete (I do not forget St. Leo), is St. Cyprian. Dr. Gore has quoted him (p. 89), but has not understood him.

St. Cyprian refers to the passage with great frequency, because it affords him proof for so many doctrines. I take first the most famous place in which he uses it, the central paragraph of his treatise on the unity of the Church. Its celebrity arises from the well-known "interpolations" which appear in many editions. I give a translation of the original form from Hartel's edition :

" All this occurs, beloved brethren, because men return not to the origin of the truth, nor seek the fountain-head, nor preserve the doctrine of the heavenly teaching. If this be considered and examined, a long treatise and arguments are not required ; the proof is easy to faith by a summary of the truth. The Lord says to Peter : " *I say unto thee, that thou art Peter, and upon this rock I will build My Church, and the gates of hell shall not*

overcome it. To thee will I give the keys of the Kingdom of heaven, and what thou shalt bind on earth shall be bound in heaven, and what thou shalt loose on earth shall be loosed in heaven. Upon one He builds His Church." *De Eccl. Cath. Unitate*, 4.

So far is clear. St. Cyprian next suggests a possible objection, and replies to it :

" And though to all the Apostles after His resurrection He gives a like power, and says : ' *As My Father hath sent Me, even so send I you : Receive ye the Holy Ghost. Whosesoever sins ye shall have remitted, they shall be remitted unto them, and whosesoever sins ye retain, they shall be retained ;* yet, that He might make unity plain, He disposed the origin of that same unity beginning from one. The other Apostles were indeed also what Peter was, endued with a like fellowship both of office and of power : but the beginning is made from unity, that the Church of Christ may be shown to be one." *Ibid.*

The meaning is clear. St. Cyprian admits that the Apostolic office and the power of binding and loosing were given alike to all, but Peter is the foundation on whom the other Apostles are built, and in whom, therefore, they have their unity. According to Dr. Gore : "This institution of the Church in the person of one man first, was a symbolic act to emphasise Christ's intention of unity. Peter, when Christ speaks to him after his great confession, is addressed as the ' representative of the Church.' " This is a mistake.

St. Augustine does, indeed, frequently say that it was as the representative of the Church and as Primate of the Apostles that St. Peter received the keys and the power of binding and loosing ; it is one of his favourite phrases, for the Donatists, against whom he wrote so much, denied that the Church had this power in the full

---

[1] St. Optatus has been quoted. Notice St. Cyprian also : " The Church, which is one, and was founded upon one, who also received the keys of it, by the voice of the Lord." *Ep.* 73, 11. The passage to be cited from St. Jerome, *Adv. Jov.* i. 26, is an exception.

sense. But he never thought of saying anything so absurd as that Peter was the representative of the Church *when he was called the rock upon which the Church is built*— as though the Church could be founded on itself! St. Augustine applied the metaphor of the rock to our Lord Himself. The powers explicitly given to St. Peter he received as the representative of the Church, because (as St. Augustine held) he was its head, nor can any other cause be imagined by which he could become its representative. To return to St. Cyprian, "a symbolic act" suggests, I am afraid, the unfortunate explanation of St. Cyprian given by Father Puller and by the late Archbishop Benson, that: "The Apostles are all made equal in honour and power by our Lord's commission. Simply to declare the unity of His Church, He, the first time that He gives that commission, gives it to one." That is to say, the great proof, according to St. Cyprian, of the unity of the Church and of mon-episcopacy, is the promise made to St. Peter alone that he should receive what, in fact, all the Apostles were to receive! Archbishop Benson naturally thought the argument a poor one.[1]

Now it is evident that St. Cyprian does not say anything of that authority which St. Peter theoretically received over the other Apostles (theoretically, I say, for no one supposes that he ordered them about). But the mention of this superiority was not to the point. What St. Cyprian wishes to emphasise is *the unity which must characterise a structure which arises on a single rock*. It is just this which makes in his eyes the im-

portance of the text, and it is just this which Anglican eyes have failed to see.

In consequence, we find St. Cyprian, almost each time he mentions St. Peter, calling him "Peter upon whom the Church is built."[2]

The same text is to the same Saint the great proof of the authority of the bishop. Obviously the government of the Church by monarchical bishops cannot be directly proved from Holy Scripture; it rests upon tradition. To St. Cyprian, as to the Fathers generally, bishops are successors of the Apostles. The powers of binding and loosing given to all the Apostles have come down to bishops. But the bishop is not thereby shown to be the one ruler of his diocese. On the contrary, one might rather infer that, as the Apostles certainly all received jurisdiction over the whole Church, so each diocese after this analogy should be governed by a college of bishops, and some scholars think this was actually the earliest system. St. Cyprian is most anxious to prove the divine origin of monepiscopacy, and he boldly bases it on our Lord's words to St. Peter :—

"Our Lord, whose precepts we ought to fear and observe, in establishing the office of a bishop and the constitution of His Church in the Gospel, speaks and says to Peter: '*I say unto thee that thou art Peter . . . be loosed in heaven.*' Hence, through the changes and successions of time, the establishment of bishops and the constitution of the Church are handed down, so that the Church is con-

---

[1] Benson, *Cyprian*, ch. iv. 1, p. 181; Puller, *Prim. SS.* 3d. ed., ch. ii. app. B., p. 88.

[2] *Ep.* 71, p. 773; *Ep.* 43, p. 594; *Ep.* 70, p. 769; *Ep.* 59, 7, p. 674; *Ep.* 66, 8, p. 732; *Ep.* 73, 7, p. 783; *Ibid.* 11, p. 786; *De hab. virg.* 10, p. 194; *Ad Fort.* 11, p. 338. I have quoted all these passages in *Revue Bénéd.* Oct. 1902, p. 370. I have used above much that I had already inserted in my three articles on St. Cyprian, *Revue Bénéd.* July, 1902, Oct., 1902, and Jan., 1903.

stituted upon bishops, and every act of the Church is directed by these same prelates." *Ep.* 33, 1.

But if the paramount and singular authority of the bishop is derived from St. Peter, it seems hard not to conclude that St. Peter himself had an authority which was singular and paramount. Let us hear another passage on episcopal authority:—

"There is one God and one Christ and one Church founded upon Peter by the voice of the Lord. Another altar cannot be established, nor a new Priesthood set up, besides the one altar and the one Priesthood. Whoso gathers elsewhere, scatters abroad." *Ep.* 43, 5.

The Chair is the episcopal office, as often in St. Cyprian. The Priesthood (*sacerdotium*) is the Episcopate. There can be but one bishop in a diocese, we are told, because our Lord set up but one Chair when He made His promise to St. Peter. Let an African bishop of the next century comment for us on this point. St. Optatus writes:—

"You cannot deny that you know that in the city of Rome the Chair was first conferred on Peter, in which the prince of all the Apostles, Peter, sat . . . in which Chair unity should be preserved by all, so that he should now be a schismatic and a sinner who should set up another Chair against that unique one." *c. Parmen.* ii. 2.

The meaning of St. Optatus is not doubtful. Peter localised his Chair in Rome, and made that the centre of unity :—

"Therefore in the Single Chair, which is the first of the endowments [enumerated by Parmenian, the writer's Donatist adversary] sat first Peter, to whom succeeded Linus . . . [a list of the Popes follows] . . . to Damasus succeeded Siricius, who is our colleague, with whom the whole world together with us is united in one fellow-

ship of communion by the interchange of letters. . . ." *c. Parm. ibid.*[1]

St. Optatus seems to have written at first in the reign of Damasus, and to have added the name of Siricius later. (Had he lived long enough, he would have added, "and to Siricius Anastasius, and to Anastasius. . . . Pius, and to Pius Leo, and to Leo Pius X., with whom the whole world together with us is united in one fellowship of communion.") St. Cyprian has the same doctrine: he calls the see of Rome "the place of Peter";[2] St. Peter, as the first of the Apostles, possessed a primacy,[3] and this primacy remained in his see; for when Novatian made himself antipope, St. Cyprian says, "He assumed the primacy."[4] The See of Rome is "the Chair of Peter, the primatial Church, whence unity had its origin."[5]

We learn from these two primi-

[1] Dr. Gore is apologetic about St. Optatus: "If Optatus, who was earlier than Augustine, seems to attribute to the see of Peter at Rome more actual authority as the centre of unity, it must be remembered that he too uses 'the see of Peter' in an ideal sense as identical with the episcopate" (he certainly does not do so in the passage before us, where he actually gives a list of the Popes !); "and if he is emphatic on the necessity of union with the see of Peter, he is as emphatic on the necessity of union with the Asiatic Churches, to whom St. John wrote." Emphatic, yes—but not "as emphatic," for he does not represent them as the *centre* of communion. St. Augustine also sometimes makes the same appeal to the Donatists' separation from *all* the Apostolic Churches. The argument was a forcible one, to bring them to a sense of their isolation. Does not Dr. Gore see that it applies with equal force to the Anglicans? *One* Apostolic Church remains untainted by heresy, and with an admittedly unrivalled history and an unbroken tradition—Dr. Gore is not in communion with it, or with any Apostolic Church.
[2] *Ep.* 55, 8.   [3] *Ep.* 71, 3.
[4] *Ep.* 69, 8.   [5] *Ep.* 59, 14.

tive African bishops, therefore, that St. Peter was by no means a mere symbol of unity, but that he received from Christ a monarchical power which is the origin of the monarchical power of bishops. This episcopal sway he himself, before any other, exercised in a particular see, and in consequence unity may be said to have taken its rise from thence. To that see he has bequeathed his primacy, and St. Optatus has told us that it remained ever the centre of the Church's unity. But St. Cyprian, beyond all doubt, held the same doctrine. When Novatian became the rival of the lawful bishop of Rome, and seemed for a moment to be about to rend the world into two factions, as was the case during the great schism of the fifteenth century, we cannot understand the history of those months, unless we realise that Rome was then universally looked upon as the centre of the Catholic Church. If this had not been so, it would have been possible and natural for bishops in different parts of the world to take opposite views as to the legitimacy of the rival bishops of Rome, without breaking off relations with one another. When Pope Stephen decided in favour of certain claimants to the sees of Leon and Asturias in Spain, while St. Cyprian thought the Pope had been deceived, and declared for their rivals, there was no reason in this for any suspension of communion between Rome and Carthage. But in the case of two claimants to the "primatial Church, the see of Peter," those who attached themselves to the wrong Pope were outside the Church of God. This is repeatedly assumed by St. Cyprian. He writes to a bishop, who had inclined to the party of Novatian, and had just told the Saint to inform Pope Cornelius that he had changed his mind :

"You also wrote that I should send a copy of the same letter to our colleague Cornelius, that he might know that you now communicate with him—that is, with the Catholic Church." *Ep.* 55, 1.

And to Cornelius himself he writes :

"We are conscious of having exhorted everyone who set sail (for Rome) . . . to recognise and hold fast the womb and root of the Catholic Church." *Ep.* 48, 3.

It is evidently assumed that not to communicate with Cornelius was to be divided from the Church. Similarly he writes to Cornelius that a common letter was sent from assembled bishops to every bishop in Africa, exhorting them "to approve firmly and hold fast thee and thy communion—that is, the unity and the charity alike of the Catholic Church".[1] This means nothing less than that the whole of Africa, with Numidia and Mauritania, containing all but a hundred dioceses —instead of condescendingly receiving Cornelius to their communion — have to congratulate themselves that they are in his communion—that is, the communion of the Catholic Church.

But what of the authority of St. Peter? I have already pointed out that he would not lord it over his brethren, but he would strive to seem their servant. But St. Cyprian makes it plain that the primacy in his time involved real powers. He tells us that when Novatian "assumed the primacy," he "sent out his new Apostles into many cities, and though in all provinces and cities there were already established bishops," he dared to create other false bishops over their heads.[2] We

---

[1] *Ep.* 48, 3.
[2] *Ep.* 55, 24.

learn from St. Dionysius of Alexandria soon after, that the Churches which had regained peace after the disturbances caused by Novatian, included Antioch, Cæsarea of Palestine, Jerusalem, Tyre, Laodicea, Tarsus, all Cilicia and Cappadocia, Syria and Arabia (where the Churches were largely assisted with contributions from Rome), Mesopotamia, Pontus and Bithynia.[1] So far did the pretensions of the Anti-Pope extend.

A few years later, the famous decree of Stephen, against which Cyprian rebelled, was a rule proposed, as by a supreme authority, to the whole Church, to be obeyed under pain of excommunication.[2] St. Cyprian did not think it a question of faith, but of discipline only, and a point on which each bishop should be free—an unpractical view —and he would not obey an order which he thought mistaken. Yet he actually said nothing against the prerogatives of the Pope in all the strong language which he "poured out against Stephen in his irritation."[3] He complained of the Pope's pride; but if he had found the decree to his taste, he would without doubt have spoken words extolling the Chair of Peter.

The length of this discussion of St. Cyprian's interpretation of the text of St. Matthew makes it necessary to pass over the other Fathers, and come at once to the next point.[4]

---

[1] Euseb. *Hist. Eccl.* vii. 5.

[2] According to Bishop Gore, Pope Stephen endeavoured to "impose conditions of communion which interfered with the Catholic liberty of other Churches" (p. 118). So St. Cyprian thought, for he held that Stephen was wrong. But in agreeing in this case with St. Cyprian, Dr. Gore is obliged to disagree with the Fathers who followed. It is clear from all St. Augustine's long discussions that he thought St. Stephen's decree perfectly natural. St. Jerome looked upon it as a final decision (c. *Lucif.* 23 and 27). St. Vincent of Lerins extols St. Stephen's action as just what was suitable to the lofty position which he held (*Commonit.* 6, see ch. vi. further on). Why does Dr. Gore choose to follow Cyprian where these great doctors desert him, and why does he desert him where they uphold him—where he teaches the unity of the Church?

[3] This is St. Augustine's expression, *De Baptismo* v. 25 (36): "I am unwilling to discuss what he poured forth against Stephen in irritation." It is instructive to notice Puller's expression for the same letters of St. Cyprian: "They are the fervent utterings of a Saint"! (*Prim. Saints*, 3d. ed., p. 69). Dr. Gore's comment is indeed marvellous: "Nor did St. Augustine in later days see in Cyprian's conduct in this matter anything but what deserved the highest commendation" (p. 119). To make this statement true, we must substitute "The Donatists" for "St. Augustine," or else "Stephen's conduct" for "Cyprian's conduct." It was the Donatists who appealed to St. Cyprian, and St. Augustine can only urge against them that St. Cyprian taught unity in the strongest form—why not follow him in his love of unity, and not in his error?—a question which he might well have put to Dr. Gore. For the rest he is careful to say nothing disrespectful to the great African martyr—he declares that he "will not discuss" what he wrote against Stephen, and suggests that "Cyprian arrived at the palm of martyrdom, so that if any cloud had arisen in his lucid mind through human frailty, it should be dispersed by the brilliant sunshine of his glorious blood." *De Bapt.* i. 18 (28).

[4] I cannot pass over Dr. Gore's indefensible treatment of a passage of Origen (*in Matt. tom.* xii. 11). Full though he is of ingenuity and mysticism, Origen never doubted, or thought his readers would doubt, the pre-eminent position of Peter. But he brings some difficulties against the view that Peter alone is the rock against which hell is powerless, or alone receives the keys, and concludes that hell will prevail against none of the Apostles or of the perfect, and that all Christians in a sense receive the keys. If Dr. Gore infers from this that Peter is not above the other Apostles, he must also infer that Peter is not above any of the perfect! But Dr. Gore in a note reproaches the late Mr. Allies with having quoted Origen as pointing out "how highly St. Peter transcends the others in power," saying that by "others" the Apostles are not meant. But they

2. THE PRIMACY CONFERRED

(John xxi. 15-7).

According to Dr. Gore, the interpretation of the Fathers is "that St. Peter is here reinstated in the Apostolic commission that his threefold denial might be supposed to have lost him; it is no peculiar dignity which is being committed to him." The first of these two propositions is perfectly correct; the second is entirely false. The Fathers look upon this threefold charge to St. Peter as reinstating him in the place he might feel he had lost—not merely in the Apostleship, therefore, but *in the primacy*. It so happens that St. Cyril of Alexandria, in the passage quoted by Dr. Gore, does not expressly mention the primacy as being restored to Peter, but only the Apostleship. But what does that prove? I have already quoted the variety of titles which this Saint gives elsewhere to St. Peter. Dr. Gore ventures to refer also to St. Augustine and St. Chrysostom. "He commends the sheep to Peter as the figure of the unity of the Church," says St. Augustine, and he bears that figure "on account of his primacy." It was only to Peter that this charge could be given, except collectively, in the plural, to all; for when given to one, the other Apostles themselves are clearly not excluded from among the sheep. Dr. Gore quotes from St. Chrysostom: "He entrusts to him the

presidency of the brethren . . . and says, 'If thou love Me, preside over the brethren.'" There cannot be any question that "the brethren" here are either the Apostles, or all the faithful including the Apostles, for the preceding words were :—

"He saith to him : Feed My sheep. Why does He pass over the others and speak of the sheep to Peter? He was the chosen one of the Apostles, the mouth of the disciples, the head of the choir;[1] for this reason Paul went up to see him rather than the others ; and also to show him that his sin had been done away. . . ." "If anyone should say, 'Why, then, was it James who received the see of Jerusalem?' I should reply that He made Peter the teacher, not of that see, but of the world" (*Hom.* 88 *in Joan.* vol. viii. pp. 477-9, (525, 6)).

Let it be remembered that St. Chrysostom considered James to be an Apostle. That the rule over the brethren means over the Apostles as well is made certain by the words, "He so wiped away the denial that he even became the first of the Apostles, and was entrusted with the whole world." And even before the day of Pentecost he acts on the commission : "'In those days Peter stood up in the midst of the disciples and said'—as being fervent, and as having the flock entrusted to his care, and as the first of the choir (or as preferred in honour) he is always the first to begin to speak."[2]

[1] Dr. Gore actually finds a distinction here between Apostles and disciples ! Does he not know that in the Gospel of St. John, on which this Father is commenting, the word 'Apostle' never occurs (it is only found once in Mt. and once in Mc.), but disciple is used instead? St. Chrysostom, like St. Luke, uses disciple and Apostle interchangeably.

[2] *Adv. Judæos* 8, 3, and *Hom.* 3 *in Acta* (i. 15). In the *Dublin Review*, January, 1903, I have collected all the evidence in St. Chrysostom's writings with regard to St. Peter. The quantity is enormous, and the result of the examination is not ambiguous.

are included, as in the former passage. Origen points out that while to Peter is promised the power of binding and loosing in "the heavens," to the other Apostles and disciples this is promised only in "heaven" in the singular (Matt. xviii. 18). This he considers a great pre-eminence for Peter—most characteristically—showing all the more forcibly his determination to answer the objection, by the very absurdity (to our notions) of his solution ! (*Ibid.* tom. xiii. 31.)

For the Western Church let us consult St. Ambrose. He tells us that here our Lord is leaving Peter to us, "as it were, the vicar of His love," and that "because he alone makes this profession, he is preferred before all" (*in Luc.* x. 175). I cannot spare space to quote others. It is well known how the Fathers regularly call Peter "the Shepherd of the flock," "he who was entrusted with the flock."

Light is thrown on this incident related by St. John from the passage in St. Luke, where St. Peter's fall and restoration are not related, but prophesied : "Simon, Simon, Satan hath desired to have you, that he might sift you as wheat : but I have prayed for thee, that thy faith fail not : and when thou art converted, strengthen thy brethren" (Lc. xxii. 31). If St. Cyril is not explicit in the former passage about the restoration of the primacy, here at least there is no ambiguity : "He *passes by* the other disciples, and comes *to the Coryphæus himself* . . . 'and thou being converted, strengthen thy brethren,' that is to say, become a support and a teacher of those who come to Me by faith" (*in Luc.* xxii. 31). Next St. Chrysostom :—

"He passed over his fall, and appointed him first of the Apostles ; wherefore He said : 'Simon, Simon,' etc." (*in Ps.* cxxix. 2).

"God allowed him to fall, because He meant to make him ruler over the whole world, that, remembering his own fall, he might forgive those who should slip in the future. And that what I have said is no guess, listen to Christ Himself saying : 'Simon, Simon,' etc." (*Hom. quod freq. conven. sit.* 5, cf. *Hom.* 73 *in Joan.* 5).

So St. Ambrose : "Peter, after being tempted by the devil, is set over the Church. The Lord therefore signified beforehand what that is, that He afterwards chose him to be the pastor of the Lord's flock. For to him he said :

'But thou, when thou art converted, strengthen thy brethren" (*in Ps.* xliii. 40).[1]

It does not seem necessary to discuss the position of St. Peter in the Acts. His exercise of his primacy there is very clear, though he does not behave as a tyrant among slaves, but as a leader among brethren.[2] But as Dr. Gore has

[1] The comment of St. Ambrose's Roman contemporary Ambrosiaster (probably a distinguished senator named Hilarius) is particularly explicit : "He constituted him to be their head, as the shepherd of the Lord's flock. For amongst other things He says to His disciples : 'Watch ye and pray, lest ye enter into temptation'; and to Peter He says : 'Behold Satan hath demanded you, that he may sift you as wheat. But I have prayed for thee, that thy faith fail not, and thou later being converted, strengthen thy brethren.' What is in doubt? He prayed for Peter, and did He not pray for James and John, not to speak of the rest? It is manifest that they are all contained in Peter ; for in praying for Peter He is seen to have prayed for all. For always in the ruler the people is reproved or praised" (*Quaest. ex novo Test.* 75, *inter Opp. S. Aug.* vol. iii.). The learned Theodoret is always an important witness. He has : "'For as I,' says He, 'did not despise thee when tossed, so be thou a support to thy brethren in trouble.' . . . So this great pillar supported the tossing world, and permitted it not to fall altogether, and made it firm, and having been ordered to feed the sheep of God, etc." (*Or. de Carit.* vol. iv. p. 689, Paris ed., 1642).

[2] Dr. Gore urges that St. Paul was absolutely equal to St. Peter in all respects (p. 84, note). St. Chrysostom, who places St. Peter so high above the other Apostles, puts St. Paul alone by his side (*in Gal.* ii. 3). He does not think, of course, that St. Paul had jurisdiction over the other Apostles, but he certainly implies that he, and he alone, was the equal of St. Peter. He is fond, at the same time, of showing the great deference of St. Paul to the elder Apostle. Like other Fathers (*e.g.* Jerome, Ambrosiaster, Theodoret) he makes much of St. Paul's humility and respect in going up to Jerusalem to visit Peter, and brings out St. Paul's witness to St. Peter's primacy. This same doctrine of the equality of Peter and Paul is also found in the very "papal" writer, Ambrosiaster. In both authors the common

spoken of the Council of Jerusalem (Acts xv.), I will notice that Peter speaks last, after the discussion, declaring the true doctrine and the will of God. James arises later to propose a practical compromise, which admits the principle laid down by Peter, while it restrains the liberty of the Gentile converts for the avoidance of scandal. The Fathers regard the speeches of both Apostles as inspired, but if they attribute the decision to one, it is to Peter. I have above cited Tertullian and Chrysostom; St. Jerome says that without doubt Peter was the originator of the decree (*Ep.* 112). Theodoret says, in his letter to St. Leo, that Paul betook himself to Peter that he might carry back from him an explanation to those who were raising questions at Antioch. Bishop Gore remarks: "His lan-guage must have had a ring of irony to one as versed in Scripture as St. Leo" (p. 84, *note*). But surely Theodoret's words describe the situation fairly well; and he was not likely to indulge in irony when he was appealing to the Pope in order to get restored to his see, after twenty years of deprivation.

One more point. Dr. Gore acknowledges that St. Chrysostom mentions that St. Peter might have appointed a new Apostle in place of Judas by his own authority. It does not seem to strike him that this is the very most extreme case of authority that can be conceived. If St. Peter could make an Apostle, what limits can be set to his power in the Church? Personally, I am inclined to think that St. Chrysostom is exaggerating. (*Hom.* 3 *in Acta*, vol. ix., pp. 33–6 (23–6), Oxf. tr., pp. 37–42.)

CHAPTER VI

THE GROWTH OF THE ROMAN CHURCH

DR. GORE was quite right in combining St. Peter's own primacy with that of his successors in a single chapter, for the argument from the one to the other is *a fortiori*. If the Fathers are right in attributing to St. Peter a real primacy, it was not without reason that Christ gave the position. If in the time of the Apostles a centre, a leader, a head was needed, how much more must

expression "princes," or "Coryphæi of the Apostles," for Peter and Paul, may have suggested the idea of some kind of equality, and this again is derived from or propagated by the connection of both Apostles with Rome. Though theoretically the primacy of the Roman bishop comes from St. Peter, yet up to the present day, in all the Papal formulæ of authority, the expression used is " by the authority of the blessed Apostles Peter and Paul."

such an office be a *sine quâ non* in later days?[1]

Protestants have always felt this. They would never have thought of denying the plain witness of Holy Scripture to the primacy of Peter, they would never have dared to throw doubt upon the unanimity of the Fathers had it not been a matter of life and death to refuse to the Apostle what they could not concede to the Pope!

[1] As the Vatican Council expresses it: " Quod autem in beato Apostolo Petro Princeps Pastorum et Pastor magnus ovium Dominus Christus Jesus in perpetuam salutem ac perenne bonum Ecclesiæ instituit, id eodem auctore in ecclesia, quae fundata super petram ad finem sæculorum usque firma stabit, jugiter durare necesse est" (*Const. de fide*, cap. ii.).

It is unnecessary to insist upon a point which is so self-evident. Our Lord founded a Church, not a school of thought—a kingdom, not a republic. He began it by the choice of one man, whom he surnamed the Rock, and upon him He built the rest. Dr. Gore's conception of the primacy of St. Peter seems to be that of the scaffolding, which is necessary for a time, but undesirable as a permanency. This was not our Lord's metaphor. A rock foundation cannot be removed when the building is complete. In what way was this rock to remain? We could not have guessed *a priori;* but if we believe in the Divine government of the Church, we can learn our Lord's intention *a posteriori* by examining history to see how He carried it into effect.

In the first days the Apostles governed the Church. But one of them, an Apostle like the rest, was leader and head.

Soon after Apostolic times we find the Church governed by bishops, who claimed to be successors of the Apostles.[1] One of them, a bishop like the rest, has an exceptional dignity, and is also regarded as the successor of Peter.

The parallel is exact. Is it a coincidence? At least the bishop of Rome, since the second century —this is allowed on all hands—has never ceased to claim that he is the successor of Peter, and that he holds a primacy over the whole Church. No other bishop has ever made such a claim. We find instances in history of this authority being resisted, but none within the Church of its being denied. The claim is true, or it is antichristian.

That St. Peter and St. Paul died at Rome is not seriously doubted.[2]

For our present purpose it is quite unimportant when St. Peter first went thither.[3] In what sense he could be called " bishop " of Rome need not trouble us either. It is obvious that in his day the local episcopate was at the very most a new conception, scarcely anywhere carried out. The simple question is this : *Did St. Peter deposit the primacy in the see of Rome?*

If we put aside for the moment the question what precise powers are implied in this primacy, it will be admitted that the Fathers of the fourth and fifth centuries give the

[1] So first Hegesippus ; then Irenæus, Tertullian, Cyprian, and all later Fathers.

[2] Dr. Gore remarks : " The earliest Father who mentions the subject, St. Irenæus, regards the Roman Church as having been founded concurrently and equally by St. Peter and St. Paul." The words " concurrently and equally " are a pure invention of Dr. Gore's ; but let this pass. Why does St. Irenæus mention both Apostles, though he is giving a list of Roman bishops? Because he is speaking of the witness of the Churches to the doctrine the Apostles had deposited in them ; it was naturally important to point out that Rome bore witness to the doctrine of *two* Apostles, and those the most glorious.

[3] Dr. Gore says : " In fact (as we find from St. Paul's epistle to the Romans) there was a considerable body of Christians at the capital before any Apostle had been among them " ; and in a note : " Rom. i. 11, 12. St. Paul had not seen them, and he would not go where any other Apostle had been before him (xv. 20, 21)." This passage is of no importance controversially, but I cannot let the statement pass without contradiction. St. Paul elaborately explains his reason for not yet having fulfilled his desire of visiting the Romans. This reason is, that he could not build upon another man's foundation—that he could not preach where an Apostle had already been. But now, as he is going to Spain, he will of necessity have the pleasure of seeing them in passing, but he will not stay. He hopes that he may be able to impart to them *some* spiritual gift; that is, he modestly says, we shall have mutual consolation. His words imply *of necessity* that some Apostle (in the large sense) had been at Rome. Tradition suggests no other name than that of Peter. I believe the tradition that this Apostle went to Rome at the beginning of the reign of Claudius can be traced to the second century.

answer with one voice: St. Peter settled the primacy at Rome, and the bishop of Rome has the first place among bishops, as St. Peter had among the Apostles.

A.

We will not, however, pass over the fragmentary evidence which is supplied by the precious remains of earlier writers. But I must premise that it would not in the least prejudice my case were there extremely little evidence to be found in the first three centuries, and this for two reasons. In the first place, because we know so little about those times. In the second place, it is not *a priori* to be expected that the Roman primacy should appear at once on the face of history developed in its modern form, or even to its full extent. St. Peter was certainly not accustomed to order the Apostles about. We should not suppose that his immediate successors would at once exhibit the full consciousness of their relation to the Church. They would be aware that Rome was the first See, and consequently the centre, and that it must share in some degree the infallibility with which Christ willed his Church to be endowed. But the precise way in which this primacy was to be brought into play, the manner and method of the exercise of Roman authority in faith and government, would need time for their unfolding. One would imagine that a whole system of canon law would be needed before it could be seen when and where the Pope ought to step in, and where the rights of the episcopate should be upheld.[1]

Now, as a fact, there has been a continual evolution of canon law with respect to these difficult questions. Different customs have obtained in different centuries. But what seems to me exceedingly striking is the fact that the whole theory which underlies all the later varieties of practice can be traced as soon as we have any evidence at all. Instead of being distressed at the small amount of evidence for the Papal claims in the earliest times, I stand amazed at the extraordinary celerity with which the Papal idea came to maturity. I have only gradually arrived at this feeling, as the result of prolonged study, and in spite of deeply rooted anticipations of the contrary. The most eminent Protestant scholars in Germany take a view of the development of the Roman Church which in some cases, I think, exaggerates its rapidity and its import. But when all allowances are made, the facts, few as they are, present us with a surprising development in an age when the relation of the Son of God to the Father, and the Divinity of the Holy Ghost (to take instances from cardinal doctrines), were ill understood, or misunderstood, or incorrectly stated, by Catholic writers. A swift sketch will illustrate my meaning.

In the first place, we have the authoritative letter of the Church of Rome to the Church of Corinth, the authorship of which is given by early and repeated testimony to

[1] It is to be observed that the words which introduce the Vatican definition, "secundum antiquam atque constantem universalis Ecclesiæ fidem" are to be understood in the sense in which they are true of every dogma of the faith. It is not meant that the belief in every part of

the Church in every century as to every detail of the Vatican definition can be demonstrated by historical proof. This could scarcely be done with regard to the unity of God or the Catholicity of the Church. It is sufficient for the proof of the antiquity of a dogma if we can trace its germ in early ages, and follow its necessary logical development, even in spite of many inconsistencies of teaching—as, for instance, in the case of the doctrine of the Incarnation.

St. Clement (*c.* 96). It is truly extraordinary to find a bishop of Rome in the lifetime of the Apostle St. John writing as a superior to a Greek Church of Apostolic foundation.[1]

A few years later St. Ignatius writes to the Church of Rome with extraordinary veneration.[2] About half a century later Dionysius, bishop of Corinth, sent a letter to the Romans,[3] in which he says that the

[1] Dr. Gore says that St. Clement "writes with a tone of considerable authority" (p. 94), but suggests that he "speaks with authority as one of the chief order—the apostolic order of bishops—writing to a Church in which as yet there were no officers higher than presbyters." But surely St. Clement was not the nearest bishop. It is curious that Dr. Gore has not further seen that this suggestion is in flat contradiction with his thesis (see his note on the following page, 95), that for two centuries "the importance of the bishop of Rome is merged in the importance of his Church." In this *one* really crucial instance of this "merging" Dr. Gore is afraid to accept the view, because of the vast authority it already implies in that Church! It is surely somewhat wild to attempt to separate this remarkable letter from the long series of "papal aggressions," of which it is, according to Bishop Lightfoot, the first instance (*Clement of Rome*, vol. i. p. 70). Dr. Gore would have done well to follow such good Protestants as Lightfoot, Harnack, Sohm, etc.
[2] St. Ignatius begins his letter to the great Church of Ephesus with a longer address than in the case of the other Asian Churches; but when he addresses Rome his magniloquence finds the Greek language insufficient, and he coins a series of long words to express his love and admiration. Also for the simple "to the Church which is in Tralles," "to the Church which is in Ephesus," etc., of the other letters he substitutes "to the Church which *presides* in the place of the region of the Romans" (the pleonasm being merely for grandeur), and adds, "who presides over the love." The explanation of this last expression by Lightfoot (so Dr. Gore, p. 94, note) "presiding in love" is improbable. I follow that of Funk. Harnack's view is impossible (see my article, *Revue Bénéd.*, 1896, and F. X. von Funk, *Kirchengesch. Abhand.*, vol. i. 1897). The meaning seems to be "presiding over the union of Christians."
[3] Ap. Euseb. *H.E.* iv. 23.

letter sent by them will be read publicly from time to time like the former one written "through Clement"; but he also speaks of the new letter as "the blessed words of Soter, your bishop," "as those of a loving father to his children." He tells us of the generous almsgiving of the Roman Church as even then (*c.* 170) a custom handed down from their fathers; so that the Roman Church is represented as having been very rich by the end of the first century. The same almsgiving is noted by St. Dionysius of Alexandria[4] in the middle of the third century; and Eusebius tells us that it remained a custom of the Roman Church up to the persecution in his own day.[5] This generosity must have assisted to increase and establish the importance of the Church of the capital.

But there is no reason to doubt that when St. Clement appealed to the martyrdom of Peter and Paul as an example of virtue[6] he was recalling a glory which, to the Christians of the second century, outshone the greatness of the Roman city and the riches of the Roman Church. St. Ignatius could not but mention the two Apostles when begging the Romans not to use the influence which some Christians seemed to have possessed in high quarters to procure the mitigation of his sentence. He says: "Not as Peter and Paul do I command you," implying that these were the former rulers of the Roman Church.[7] About the year 180 the true glory of the Roman Church is described by St. Irenæus in a celebrated passage, and there is no possible doubt but that he echoes the feeling of those idealist days. The early Church did not bow down before

[4] Ep. 5, Ap. Euseb. *H.E.* vii. 5.
[5] iv. 23. [6] *Ad. Cor.* 5.
[7] *Ad. Rom.* 4.

power and wealth alone, as Protestants imply. The greatness of
the capital was one element in the
development of the Papal power,
but the connection with Peter and
Paul was both the germ and the
most potent influence (iii. 3).

" But since it would be very long in
a volume of this sort to give the
successions of all the Churches, we
will point to that of the exceedingly
great and ancient Church which was
founded and established at Rome by
the most glorious Apostles Peter and
Paul. By its tradition and by its 'faith
announced to men' (*Rom.* i. 8), which
has been transmitted to us by the
successions of bishops, we confound
all those who in any way, by caprice
or vain glory, or by blindness and perversity of will, gather where they ought
not."

Here the greatness of the Church
is its antiquity, its foundation by
the princes of the Apostles, and its
praise by St. Paul. The passage
which follows is difficult, but it is
at least certain that it has no reference to the secular greatness of the
city.

" For to this Church, on account of
its more powerful principality (*prop-
ter potentiorem principalitatem*), it is
necessary that every Church, that is,
the faithful from all sides, should come
together (agree), in which the tradition
from the Apostles has always been
preserved by those that are from all
parts."

" In which " may refer either to
the Church of Rome or to " every
Church." It is just possible to make
principalitas = ἀρχαιότης (ἄρχη =
principium, ἀρχαῖος = *principalis ;*
hence ἀρχαιότης = *principalitas*).
Convenire may mean " agree " or
" resort." In any case the comparative *potentior* seems to compare
the headship (or antiquity, origin)
with that of other leading Churches;
and the cause of this superiority
is clearly the foundation by " the

most glorious Apostles," which had
been mentioned in the first place of
all.[1] The result of this superiority
is that other Churches *must agree
with its tradition*, or *must resort to
it*. This has always seemed to me
to be a very tremendous testimony
to the position of the Roman Church
in St. Irenæus's day. He goes
on :—

" The Blessed Apostles therefore
having founded and built the Church,
entrusted to Linus the office of bishop
. . . and Anencletus succeeds him . . .
(*a list follows*) . . . and Soter having

[1] Dr. Gore's exposition of this passage
is one which is followed by many Catholics
and Protestants. The Church of Rome
has a " microcosmic" character, because
all the faithful necessarily resort thither.
This is quite inconsistent with the context,
in which it is the unbroken tradition from
Peter and Paul, proved by the enumeration of bishops, which is an unanswerable
proof against the heretics. I do not think
it would suffice to urge that this latter
argument is borrowed from Hegesippus
(as it is), and that St. Irenæus has strength-
ened it by an incongruous addition, for
the whole preceding paragraph, and the
whole argument, from the beginning of
the book, implies the argument from the
succession. For this reason I prefer to
take *convenire* = " agree." But on page 95
Dr. Gore has a note in which he says of
the passage : " I believe that Dr. Langen,
following Grabe and Neander, has finally
fixed its meaning." Now Dr. Langen's
view is that *potentior principalitas* refers
to the city, not to the Church ; it is not
from the greatness of its Church ; but because it is the capital, that Rome is
" resorted to " by Christians. I hope Dr.
Gore does not accept this impossible view,
which has been abandoned by Father
Puller in the third edition of his *Primitive
Saints*, and which is unsupported by any
critics. It is violent to translate " to this
Church on account of the powerful headship of its city," and it is also violent to
distinguish the " headship" from the praise
which has gone before—antiquity, faith,
Apostolic foundation. The late Dr. Bright,
in spite of his prejudice against anything
" Roman," rejected this view, and I am
glad that it is not clear that Dr. Gore
accepts it. Dr. Langen always writes with
the bitterness of a partisan against the
Church.

succeeded Anicetus, now in the twelfth place from the apostles Eleutherus holds the lot of the Episcopate. In the same order and in the same teaching (*or* succession) the tradition of the Church from the Apostles and the preaching of the truth has come down to us. And this is a most complete proof that it is one and the same life-giving faith which has been preserved in the Church from the Apostles until now, and handed down in truth."

Similarly in Tertullian we find not a trace of the greatness of the Roman city, but he exclaims: "How happy that Church into which the Apostles poured forth all their faith with their blood!"[1] It is the Apostolic origin, and that consequent gift of faith to which St. Ignatius also refers, which is the glory of Rome in his eyes.

Our knowledge of the second century is unfortunately but a succession of small scraps. We know various out-of-the-way details, but of the everyday life of Christians and of the constitution of the Church we hear little or nothing. Yet we find that Rome was throughout that century, so far as we can tell, the centre of Church life; in fact, we do not learn much of any other Church, except for glimpses of those of Asia Minor. The second century is chiefly remarkable for the broods of heretics it brought forth, and of these we often know more than we do of the Catholics whom they opposed. Most of these teachers and their disciples came to Rome to make proselytes, "but," says Caspari, "they desired besides to gain importance in the great, highly thought of, and very influential Church community of the capital of the world, and, indeed, partly to obtain recognition from her, in order thereby to get easier access elsewhere, and to be enabled to spread with more

force. The dignity of the Church of Rome was to cover them in their efforts; she was, so to speak, to stamp them with the hall-mark of Christianity and Catholicity, or orthodoxy." So far this illustrious Protestant scholar.[2] Valentinus came to Rome under Pope Hyginus (*c.* 140), and Cerdo came about the same time, and after him Marcion. Thus the first two heresies of any importance, Valentinianism and Marcionism, tried to make the Church of Rome their headquarters. Under Anicetus came Marcellina, foundress of the Carpocratians (*c.* 160). Two priests of Rome, Florinus and Blastus, were deposed by Pope Eleutherius for their heretical teaching. Before and after the year 200 came Apelles and Potitus, Basiliscus and Syneros, and a crowd of "Adoptianists" and Monarchians. Under Eleutherius, Theodotus, the leather-seller of Byzantium, was in Rome with his disciples Asclepiodotus, Hermophilus, and Theodotus the banker, who was excommunicated by the next Pope, Victor. This sect made the first anti-Pope. They got hold of a confessor called Natalius, and bribed him to be their bishop, at a salary of 150 denarii a month. He was warned by visions not to consent, but not having hearkened to them, "he was beaten all night by the holy angels" (so we are informed by a contemporary writer), so that in the morning he was fain to put on sackcloth and ashes, and cast himself weeping at the feet of Pope Zephyrinus, and "with many prayers and showing the marks of the stripes, he was with difficulty restored to communion."[3]

Another follower of Theodotus, Artemon, was probably in Rome,

---

[1] *De Præscr.*, xxxvi. (quoted by Dr. Gore, p. 95).

[2] *Quellen zur Geschichte des Tauf-Symbols*, vol. iii. pp. 309–48. In the following pages I have drawn upon Caspari's account.

[3] Ap. Euseb., *H. E.*, v. 28.

C

and to Rome about 180 came the leader of the Monarchians, Praxeas, and after him came Epigonus, Cleomenes, and the more famous Sabellius, with whom we dip some twenty years into the next century. About the same time took place at Rome a famous discussion between a certain Caius and Proclus the Montanist. Long before this, Pope Soter is said to have issued a writing against Montanism, and Eleutherius or Victor, after seeming to favour the Montanists (so says Tertullian), condemned them.[1]

If we turn to the first quarter of the third century we find the rigorist doctrines of Montanists and others condemned by Zephyrinus and Callistus. From Syria to Rome come the Elkesaites, Alcibiades of Apamea arriving after the martyrdom of Pope Callistus.

In the second century orthodox teachers also came to Rome. Besides St. Ignatius, who came in bonds, we have St. Justin Martyr, his disciple Tatian, afterwards a heresiarch, and Tatian's disciple Rhodon. St. Polycarp came to Rome under Pope Anicetus when more than eighty years of age. St. Irenæus came thither as envoy of the Church of Lyons. Tertullian naturally visited Rome. Thus the ecclesiastical writers of the day came to the city or were natives of it (Victor, Hippolytus, Gaius).

These details which we can glean from the few sparse notices of the period which remain to us are an interesting commentary on the words of St. Irenæus as to the *potentior principalitas* of Rome. We know that Rome was the capital. We know also that it was the see of Peter in the opinion of the Christian world. It is open to Dr. Gore to put down all the influence of the Roman Church to the former of these two facts and to brand the Christians as men of worldly views who thought much of the Imperial Court and nothing of the prince of the Apostles. I myself prefer to see in the position accorded to Rome the reverence for Peter and Paul, as, indeed, Dionysius of Corinth and Irenæus have assured us, though I see in the facility of communication with Rome the divinely intended means of developing her primacy in fact.

So far, we have seen Rome simply as a great centre of Church life, and positive action of the Popes has only appeared in the letter of Clement and in the condemnation of heretics. About 196–7 a phase of the Paschal question affords us a brilliant flash of light upon the relations of Rome with foreign Churches, a subject on which it must be remembered that our information is otherwise practically nil for this period.

Pope Victor initiates a movement in favour of unity of observance. Councils are simultaneously held at his request [2] throughout Christendom, and all publish decisions that Easter must be celebrated only on Sunday. The Asiatic Churches

---

[1] Tertullian, when a Montanist, writes as follows :—" For when the Bishop of Rome (Victor ?) was just acknowledging the prophecies of Montanus, Prisca, and Maximilla, and by that very recognition was bringing peace to the Churches of Asia, Praxeas, by telling falsehoods about the prophets and their Churches, and defending the precedents set by the bishop's predecessors, induced him to revoke the letters of peace which he had already sent and to recede from his intention of accepting the truth of the gifts" (c. Prax. 1). The Montanists, it appears, tried to get their "gifts" approved at Rome. Asia was disturbed and divided. The news that the Pope was sending letters of peace to the Montanist prophets and their Churches was sufficient to unite the orthodox with them and to bring peace to the Churches of Asia. This is an illuminating episode.

[2] Or "order," cp. "οὓς ὑμεῖς ἠξιώσατε μετακληθῆναι ὑπ' ἐμοῦ," Euseb., *H. E.*, v. 24.

alone resist this decision. St. Victor "tries to cut them off from the common unity." Some other bishops think this too harsh, for the Bishop of Ephesus had pleaded a tradition received from the Apostle St. John, and they "took Victor to task somewhat sharply." Amongst these St. Irenæus "becomingly" [1] urged Victor to consider that the difference in the custom of the fast only brought the unity of faith more clearly into relief. Especially he dwelt upon the precedent set by the former Popes in permitting the divergence.[2] Eusebius, who is our sole informant (*H. E.*, v. 24), cannot relate the sequel. It is pretty certain that, not only in the time of Tertullian's Montanist writings, but some three years after these events, when he wrote his *De Præscriptionibus*, there was no division between Rome and Asia. Did Victor give way, as we should expect, when he found that his action was not popular nor effective? Or is it possible that Asia relinquished her peculiarity then and there at the sight of the consensus against her? She altered her custom at some time, and it may well have been now, as we hear of no further troubles.

However this may be, we find in this incomplete story a Pope conscious that it is he who is to see to uniformity in the Christian Churches. We see councils assembled everywhere at his demand. We see him claim to have the right to excommunicate not, as before, merely individual heresiarchs, but numerous and populous Churches of Apostolic foundation. His action "did not please all the bishops," so we see that many were, in fact, satisfied. But he was precipitate, and naturally drew down remonstrances upon his head, and was unable to carry out his intention. Dr. Gore seems to think this implies that his right was not recognised. There is no trace of any denial of the right, but only of the justice of its exercise. It is particularly to be noticed that St. Irenæus's argument is based on the practice of Victor's predecessors. I must admit that *a priori* I should not have expected the papal authority to have reached so high a point of evolution at so early a date, but our information, though meagre, is precise. Taken together with the rest of the few contemporary facts which bear upon the subject, the Papacy appears as a practical factor of the first importance in Church life, and not as a mere theoretical primacy, as we might well have anticipated.

We need not dwell long upon the third century. We learn from Tertullian that Pope Callistus issued a decree on the subject of penance to the whole Church, "this bishop of bishops and Pontifex Maximus," as the heretic derisively entitles him. The author of the *Philosophumena* makes this Pope answerable for the appointment of persons who had married twice to the Episcopate.[3] Under Zephyrinus Origen went to Rome, "desiring to see the most ancient Church of the Romans."

---

[1] Eusebius, who had no manner of sympathy with the Asiatics, apparently contrasts this with the "somewhat sharply" or "too sharply," πληκτικώτερον, of the rest.

[2] Compare the action of Praxeas in appealing to papal precedents (p. 66 above, note).

[3] *Phil.* ix. 12. Dr. Gore thinks it a luminous fact that the author of this treatise accuses his contemporary, Pope Callistus, with teaching of heresy. But the writer clearly shows that whether he is Hippolytus or not, he is an anti-Pope. Surely it is neither remarkable nor illuminating to find a pretender accusing the true Pope of being a heresiarch *ex cathedra*. It seems to me that a little consideration would have enabled Dr. Gore to shorten his book to an appreciable extent.

We have already heard enough of St. Cyprian's views,[1] but it is now apparent how they fall into line with the rest of the evidence. The peremptory decree of Stephen was similar in character to those of Victor and of Callistus. How many more there must have been of which we have no record, and how familiar such Papal action must have been in St. Cyprian's day !

The great St. Dionysius of Alexandria was accused of heretical teaching. It was to his only superior in the Church, his namesake, Dionysius of Rome, that he appealed. Our informant is his successor, Athanasius,[2] who himself made a like appeal. When Paul of Samosata, bishop of Antioch, was deposed by an Eastern council, he kept possession of the episcopal residence, relying on the protection of Queen Zenobia. The matter was brought before the civil courts, and the heathen emperor, Aurelian, decided that the house should be made over to whichsoever party was recognised by the bishops of Italy and Rome, that is, the Pope and his Council.[3] It had clearly been pleaded that the test of orthodox communion lay in union with the centre.

B.

We have now before us a slight sketch of the anti-Nicene evidence on our subject. Many less important points might of course be added, but we have heard enough for the purpose in hand.

We saw in chapter ii. that the Church was founded upon Peter for the sake of unity of government, and that this unity is threefold—of faith, of communion, of government. We have found Rome to be very

clearly the centre of unity in these precise points. St. Irenæus explicitly declares her to be the centre of faith and communion. St. Cyprian is equally distinct. As guardian of the faith she is attacked by all the heresies, and condemns them all in turn. She is appealed to as judge of faith by St. Dionysius, bishop of the second see of Christendom. Her government we see in action in the masterful words of Clement, of Victor, of Callistus, of Stephen. We have not a finished picture, we cannot fill in all the details, but the general effect is vivid enough. The least we can conclude, I think, is that the Church already universally recognised in the Roman Church a leadership, an authority, the exercise of which might be annoying, or to be resisted in some cases, but which was nevertheless lawful and necessary, and derived from no worldly rank or wealth, but from the succession to Peter and Paul.

In Germany Protestant scholars have been greatly struck by the development of the Church of Rome in the second century. The well-known excursus, "Catholic and Roman," in the second volume of Harnack's *History of Dogma*, is typical and easy of access. He is prejudiced against "Catholicism," which is, in his view, a mere superstition, a travesty of the rationalist Christianity without a Christ which he professes. He tries to minimise some of the witnesses to the greatness of the Roman Church (for instance, those afforded by Ignatius and Irenæus), but he holds that these two disagreeable elements, "Roman" and "Catholic," were identical from the beginning. I do not agree with every one of the proofs which he gives, e.g. I do not believe that Rome had much to do with the earliest collections of New Testament books or originated the

[1] Above, ch. v.
[2] *De decretis Nicænæ Synodi*, 25, *De Sententia Dionysii*, 13.
[3] Euseb., *H. E.*, vii. 30.

idea of a "canon," but in general it must be admitted that his results are to be accepted, as, in fact, in Germany they are accepted.

"Now it is an *a priori* probability that this transformation of Christianity [into an organised Catholic Church], which was simply the adaptation of the gospel to the then existing empire, came about under the guidance of the metropolitan Church, the Church of Rome ; and that 'Roman' and 'Catholic' had therefore a special relation from the beginning" (p. 150). "It can, however, be proved that it was in the Roman Church, which, up to about the year 190, was closely connected with that of Asia Minor, that all the elements on which Catholicism is based first assumed a definite form" (p. 151). " From these considerations we can scarcely doubt that the fundamental Apostolic institutions and laws of Catholicism were framed in the same city that in other respects imposed its autority on the whole earth, and that it was the centre from which they spread, because the world had become accustomed to receive law and justice from Rome" (p. 155). Again, after an exposition of the arguments : "All these causes combined to convert the Christian communities into a real confederation under the primacy of the Roman Church (and subsequently under the leadership of her bishops)" (p. 160).

Now Dr. Harnack is clearly under the impression that he has established an anti-Catholic thesis. He emphasises the influence of the capital, and represents the reference to Peter as a later notion. Still more he holds, like Dr. Gore (p. 95, note), that the greatness of the Roman bishop is a subsequent idea. In fact, he (quite unreasonably and absurdly) holds that at Rome alone, of all important Churches, there was actually no bishop at all until after the middle of the second century ![1]

[1] Harnack, *Chronologie*, i. pp. 172 foll. I have replied in *Revue Bénéd.*, Avril, 1902, pp. 149 foll.

Few people are likely to follow him in this wild theory. But apart from this his view is entirely acceptable to Catholics, and has much in its favour.

Let us consider for a few moments. God being almighty, it would have been easy for Him to establish an efficient headship of His Church at Timbuctoo or anywhere else had He so willed. But He does not habitually employ extraordinary means where ordinary ones are at hand for the accomplishment of His purposes. It was therefore natural that He should fix the centre of the new world-wide faith at Rome. Every road in those days led to Rome. The communications of the Empire ramified from thence like nerves from the brain and arteries from the heart. The Fathers tell us that Peter fixed his seat in Rome. This was a masterly stroke of divine strategy by which the Church in its infancy was enabled to reap the full benefit of the fulness of times which God had preordained for her birth and growth. Jerusalem was to perish. The headquarters of the Christian army are shifted from Jerusalem to Rome, and in one move it is proclaimed that the new religion is not for one race, but for the world. The last and greatest of the world empires of prophecy, the power which was to crush Israel with the final blow, was to be besieged by Christianity in its own citadel. To preach a world-wide religion in the capital of the world —we see how this idea caught the imagination of St. Paul, and only the knowledge that an Apostle had preceded him could keep him back. But God's plans were not as his, and in spite of himself the Apostle of the Gentiles preached Christ in Rome, but in bonds, and suffered there with his senior Apostle.

The Catholic theory is therefore this—

(1) Rome being the capital of the empire,

(2) St. Peter, Prince of the Apostles,

(3) Founded a Church there,

(4) The bishop of which should succeed to his primacy.

Divine providence also willed that St. Paul should join St. Peter at Rome, and that both should, with their blood, consecrate Rome to be the focus of the faith they preached.

Notice the logical order. The primary fact is the secular rank of the city, as the Eastern Fathers saw, for this was the determining cause of Peter's choice. But the principal fact is the consequent placing of the primacy in Rome by Peter. It is therefore true that Rome has the primacy, because it was the imperial city, but it is obvious that this fact could not directly give it ecclesiastical jurisdiction, but that its legitimate authority is from Peter, and from Christ through him.

Notice once more that the Pope is successor of Peter because he is Bishop of Rome; he is not Bishop of Rome because he is Pope. His position comes to him from his Church. We call the Church of Rome the mother and mistress of all Churches, and we habitually speak of "Rome" when we mean papal authority.

From all this we see how the centrality and the imposing prestige of the capital was intended to be a means for the easy development of the primacy and an assistance to the propagation of the faith. Nothing can be more obvious, therefore, than that Harnack's view is in itself reasonable if it is well founded —and in some respects I think it

is—that "the fundamental Apostolic institutions and laws of Catholicism were framed in the same city that in other respects imposed its authority on the whole earth." But let us remember that in this the great rationalist critic is going beyond what Catholics ordinarily hold with regard to the early influence of Rome. At any rate, Dr. Harnack's conclusion is not to be passed over :

"The proposition" ("the Roman Church always had the primacy") "and the statement that 'Catholic' virtually means 'Roman Catholic' are gross fictions, when devised in honour of the temporary occupant of the Roman see" [This is meaningless. Of course, every bishop is the representative of his Church and the depository of its prerogatives] "and detached from the significance of the Eternal City in profane history [no reasonable person would think of doing such a thing]; but applied to the Church of the Imperial capital, they contain a truth, the denial of which is equivalent to renouncing the attempt to explain the process by which the Church was unified and catholicised" (p. 168).[1]

[1] Dr. Gore quotes from the late Dr. Salmon, "How all through the first two centuries the importance of the Bishop of Rome is merged in the importance of his Church" (p. 95, note). It would not be surprising if this were to some extent true. We might expect the primacy of the bishop to appear as a blossom after the leaves, and that the greatness of the city would be the chief factor at first in the development. As a fact, however, there are only two instances of this supposed "merging" : (1) That St. Clement writes in the name of his Church, and does not name himself; (2) that St. Ignatius does not mention the bishop when he writes to Rome. Now there is strong reason for thinking that this omission of the name was a prudential measure, necessary in a time of persecution (see *Journal of Theol. Studies*, July, 1904, p. 530), but in any case we must remember that St. Ignatius was the last

It is interesting to find that a special gift of faith was attributed by the Fathers to the Roman Church. The bishop of that Church was early recognised to have, as one of his principal prerogatives, the special duty of upholding the faith and of condemning heresy. The Church of Rome, being his Church, is represented as sharing in the charisma of being a touchstone for heresy. As the necessary centre of Christendom, its own faith was held to be infallible. The text of St. Paul to the Romans, "Your faith is proclaimed throughout the whole world" (i. 8), was commonly quoted in this connexion. We have seen it in St. Irenæus : " The Church of Rome . . . and its faith announced to men." Long before this, St. Ignatius had spoken of the faith of the Romans as " filtered clear from every foreign stain" (*Ad Rom.* 1). At Rome, says Tertullian, the Apostles poured forth all their faith with their blood (*Præscr.* 36). The Roman clergy

write to St. Cyprian in 250, "For the Apostle had not proclaimed such high praise of us, saying, ' Your faith is declared throughout the whole world,' were it not that our vigour of to-day has its roots in those days " (*Ap.* Cypr., *Ep.* 30). St. Cyprian writes to Pope Cornelius in the same year of the Decian persecution : " With one spirit and one voice the whole Roman Church made confession. Gloriously, beloved Brother, did that faith then appear, which the Apostle praised concerning you " (*Ep.* 60, 2) ; and again, " They dare to set sail and carry letters from schismatics and profane persons to the Chair of Peter, the primatial Church, whence the Unity of the Church had its rise ; and they do not consider that those are the Romans whose faith was lauded by the praise of the Apostle, *and to whom unfaith can have no access* " (*Ep.* 59, 14).

This has been already quoted ; and so have the words of St. Gregory Nazianzen (p. 33). St. Jerome is fond of this point, for he was baptised at Rome. Here are a few quotations :

" It is the faith of the Romans which the Apostle praises. Where else do men run with the same love and the same crowds to the churches and the tombs of the Martyrs ? Where does the Amen so resound like the thunder of heaven, and the temples of the idols are shaken ? Not that the Romans have another faith than that of all the Churches of Christ, but that they have more devotion, and more simplicity in believing"(*Comm. in Gal.*, Introd.)

" Know that Roman faith, which was praised by the voice of the Apostle receives not these jugglings" (c. Ruf. iii. 12).

" What does he call his faith ? That which the Roman Church possesses ? Or that which is contained in the volumes of Origen ? If he answers 'the Roman,' then we are Catholics,

person to "merge" the authority of a bishop in that of his Church, so that we have only one case left as even a possible instance, and I confess I should be afraid to build upon it. Dr. Gore does not build upon it (as we have seen), but takes the letter to be precisely the authoritative action of a bishop towards a community governed by presbyters ! The grounds for Dr. Salmon's view are therefore very shadowy, even in the first century. For the middle and end of the second century his statement is absurd. The arrivals of the Gnostic heretics were dated, before St. Irenæus, by the Popes under whom they arrived at Rome or flourished. St. Irenæus himself only mentions the Church of Rome for the sake of giving a list of its bishops. Of the Popes of the early part of the century all record but date has perished ; but Anicetus, Soter, Eleutherus, Victor, in the second half, are more than names, and their importance is certainly not " merged in the importance of their Church," as Harnack himself testifies. It is a pity that Dr. Gore should quote such careless and incorrect statements, even though emanating from a really eminent scholar.

who have not been infected with the errors of Origen !" (*Ibid.*, i. 4).

"The Roman Faith, in which the Church of Alexandria glories in participating" (*Ep.* 63, to Theophilus, patriarch of Alex.).

"Whosoever thou art who teachest new doctrines, I beg thee, spare Roman ears, spare that faith which was praised by the Apostle's voice. Why after four hundred years dost thou try to teach us what we knew not before? Why dost thou publish what Peter and Paul would not proclaim? Until this day the world has been Christian without this doctrine. In my old age I will hold the faith in which I was regenerated when a boy." (*Ep.* 84).

Many other instances might be given from this one Father. The Roman form of the Apostles' Creed attained a special rank on account of "Roman Faith." The Council of Milan in 390 says, "Let the symbol of the Apostles be believed, which the Roman Church ever guards and preserves without alteration."[1] St. Ambrose says, "It is the symbol which the Roman Church holds, where the first of the Apostles had his seat, and brought thither the common decision of the Apostles."[2] Rufinus also assures us that the Church of Rome alone kept the creed without addition.[3]

It is unnecessary to trace this view any further (*e.g.* in St. Augustine, or the fifth century in St. Leo and Theodoret)[4] for it becomes too closely connected with the faith of the Papacy itself, and also we have been dealing till now with the first three centuries only.

C.

The fourth century affords us a great deal more evidence, though

[1] *Ap* Ambros., *Ep.* 42.
[2] *Expositio symboli ad initiandos*, no doubt a genuine piece. I use the text given by Caspari, *Alte und Neue Quellen*, p. 220.
[3] *In Symb. Ap.* 3.
[4] See an article of mine, "Fides Romana," in *Revue Bénéd*, 1895, pp. 546 foll.

still imperfect, scattered, and unequal. We must be content with a few points only, as this chapter has already reached an excessive length. Of St. Athanasius and the Arian struggles something was said in chapter iii.[5] But we cannot pass

[5] When Pope Liberius "abandoned Athanasius and notified that he had separated him from his communion, St. Athanasius betrays no other feeling than that of sorrow at the fall of a good man and anxiety to palliate his weakness." So Dr. Gore has been led by Protestant historians to believe (pp. 99, 100), and he naturally concludes: "Now we contend that if anything in the world can be certain, it is certain that St. Athanasius, had he had any idea of the Bishop of Rome being in a unique sense the guardian of the faith, much more any notion of his infallibility, must have adopted another tone in regard to his fall. He must have quivered at the awful shock of finding himself deserted by the 'Holy Father' on the central dogma of the faith. It must have been much more to him than his desertion by Hosius. There is no avoiding or palliating this conclusion." Dr. Gore gives no sign of having read the additional chapters (89, 90) to St. Athanasius's Apology, in which that saint relates what he knew of the fall of the Pope and of Hosius. He is there replying to the triumphant boasts of his enemies that his two influential supporters had now disowned him. Athanasius was well aware that he would be indeed helpless if this were true. He argues that the approval and protection they had always given him was emphasised and not weakened by their having endured exile and punishment rather than betray his cause and that of the Nicene faith. Only great sufferings had at last broken their resolution, and their fall is a disgrace to their Arian persecutors, and not a condemnation to Athanasius. This is the cause of St. Athanasius's "anxiety to palliate" both Liberius and Hosius. Though Hosius was personally of extraordinary influence and fame, yet it will be found that St. Athanasius always treats Liberius as the more important, whenever the two are mentioned. It was no doubt "a shock" to find that they had fallen; but it would have been disastrous to St. Athanasius to admit, in the only place where he mentions their fall, that it made him "quiver." It is certain, "if anything in the world can be certain," that he regarded the Pope as "being in a unique sense the

over the Council of Sardica, as Bishop Gore has referred to it.

This council met apparently in the summer of 343,[1] by the agreement of the Emperors of East and West. The place chosen was on the borders between the two parts of the Empire, and was just within the dominions of the Catholic Emperor of the West, Constans, though only some fifty miles from Constantinople, the capital of the Arianising Constantius. This was disastrous for the Eusebians, the enemies of Athanasius, who could do nothing without a "Count" (as St. Athanasius tells us) to control the proceedings in their favour. To the number of seventy-six they shut themselves up in a palace, and demanded that the deposition of Athanasius and Marcellus of Ancyra should be accepted without discussion, repeating their old refrain that one council had no right to revise the acts of another. This amounted to a denial of the right of the Pope and his Roman council to try the case once decided at Tyre, and practically refused all opportunity of redress to St. Athanasius. The rest of the bishops, probably about ninety-four or ninety-six, refused to agree to this demand, and the Easterns retired in a body, on the plea that the development of the Persian war of Constantius rendered it impossible for them to be away from their flocks. But in fact they stopped just within the border of the Eastern Empire at Philippopolis. The orthodox bishops acquitted Athanasius and Marcellus.

guardian of the faith," and I cannot see that there is any room for controversy on this point. What conception he may have had of "papal infallibility" is quite another matter, for the dogma was obviously not wholly developed in the fourth century. But the fall of Liberius under persecution has nothing to do with infallibility.

[1] So Gwatkin, *Studies*, p. 124.

They wrote to the whole Church, to the Church of Alexandria, to the bishops of Egypt,[2] and to the Pope,[3] to announce their decisions. The heretical assembly, on the other hand, excommunicated the Pope, as *princeps et dux malorum*, and addressed their synodical letter to the intruded bishop of Alexandria and to the Donatist bishop of Carthage, among others, so far from all decency had they receded.

The orthodox wrote to Pope Julius that they had felt his presence among them, in spite of his unavoidable absence from the council. They say that it will be "most proper and fitting if the bishops from all provinces shall refer to the head, that is to the see of Peter." In each of their letters the refusal of the Eusebians to obey the Pope's former summons to Rome is signalised among their errors. But it is the canons with which we have chiefly to do.

The hope of orthodoxy was in the West, for the Eastern Emperor Constantius was the support of the Arianising party, while Constans in the West was orthodox, and so were the Western bishops, almost without exception. The Bishop of Rome had exercised his prerogative in annulling the Council of Tyre, which had condemned Athanasius,[4] in sum-

[2] These letters are preserved by Athanasius in his Apology.

[3] In St. Hilary's fragments.

[4] It is important to remember that the very "papal" letter of Pope Julius to the Eusebian party has been preserved for us by St. Athanasius as the most important document of his Apology. It would be simply an absurdity to suppose that he thought any of the Pope's claims to be excessive, and in fact his case rested upon their validity. I will quote one sentence from the letter : "For if really, as you say, they [Athanasius and Marcellus] did some wrong, the judgement ought to have been given *according to the ecclesiastical canon, and not thus. You should have written to all of us, that so justice might have been decreed*

moning the patriarch of Alexandria and his accusers alike to Rome, and in restoring the ejected bishops to their sees. The question before the Fathers of Sardica was how to avoid such evils for the future. The leading bishops of the East were of the Court party, or mere creatures of the Emperor. The patriarchal sees of Alexandria and Antioch were in the hands of Arians of the worst reputation. In ordinary cases a bishop would be judged by his metropolitan and comprovincials. In the East an orthodox bishop would evidently have little chance of a hearing. An appeal to a patriarch would be yet more surely

by all. For it was bishops who were the sufferers, and it was not obscure Churches which suffered, but Churches which were ruled by Apostles in person. With regard to the Church of Alexandria in particular, why did you not consult us? Do you not know that this has been the custom, first to write to us, and so for that which is just to be defined from hence"? (Athan. *Apol.* 35). Here Julius assumes that the patriarchal sees have no superior but the Pope, and that the synod of Tyre had no power to condemn bishops without appeal. The words *in italics* do not simply mean that West must combine with East in so important a matter, but principally that *the Pope* must not be left out. This is seen in the Pope's actions and claims, and to the Greek historians of the fifth century it was so natural a conclusion that they thus paraphrase his words : "Since the ecclesiastical canon orders that the Churches shall not make canons against the opinion of the bishop of Rome" (Socrates, ii. 17), "saying that it was a sacerdotal law, that what was done against the will of the Roman bishop was null and void" (Sozomen, iii. 10, probably copying Socrates). Here they are quoting the letter of Julius, but their own view was the same ; and Socrates says in his own person (ii. 8), " Nor was Julius present (at the Council of Antioch), the bishop of great Rome, although the ecclesiastical canon orders that the Churches may make no decisions without the approval of the bishop of Rome." This is a perfectly clear statement of the Church's law as understood at Constantinople in the middle of the fifth century by learned writers.

disastrous, and the appeal to Rome in person would be a flight and a self-inflicted exile. There was certainly no doubt in the minds of the orthodox party at Sardica that the Pope could summon a patriarch to Rome, could order a council to be held, and could restore bishops to their sees by the prerogative of his see, and could quash the proceedings of any council, however large, if he had sufficient reason. All these things had lately been seen in act. But the canons agreed to at Sardica go much further than this. They initiate a new system of canon law. It was not difficult for the Easterns to avoid coming to Rome when summoned; it was a long journey, and communication was slow, and delays and excuses were easily made. This new and extraordinary system provided that if a bishop had been condemned, and had complained of injustice, it should be open to his judges, or to the bishops of the neighbouring province, or to himself, to appeal to the bishop of Rome to order a fresh trial *by neighbouring bishops*, with or without the assistance of a papal envoy or plenipotentiary. The inquiry would thus be held on the spot, or close by, and there would be no opportunity of evasion.[1]

[1] These canons have given rise to interminable discussions, but the following seems to be certainly their meaning (I follow the text given by C. H. Turner, *Journal of Theol. Studies*, April, 1902) : 1. If a bishop has been condemned, and he thinks he has a good case, let his judges or (if they will not) the bishops of the neighbouring provinces write to the Roman bishop, who will either confirm the first decision, or order a new trial, appointing the judges himself. On the motion of St. Gaudentius, bishop of Brescia, it was added that when any bishop had appealed to Rome, no successor should be appointed until the matter had been settled by the bishop of Rome. This somewhat obvious rider was directed against the deeds of the Eusebians. 2. Further, if a bishop should,

Let us notice that nothing is said about the power of the Pope to try at Rome a bishop who appealed to him ; this was an undoubted right which had recently been exercised. Let us also remark that the Pope's action is left as free as possible, " as his wisdom shall think fit." Again we have to notice that, if the Pope should send a legate or judges, he may delegate to them his own authority — this assumes that the Pope has superior authority in every province. Lastly we find that all this new legislation, founded on the admitted prerogatives of the Pope, is spoken of as an honour to St. Peter the Apostle.[1] It was not, then, the capital that these defenders of orthodoxy were honouring, but the see of the Prince of the Apostles.

The system was too extraordinary and too contrary to old custom and to the established rights of the Eastern (and even of the Western) Churches to be of any practical use. These famous canons defined a novel exercise of papal jurisdiction which never seems to have been employed. So long as the Emperor

Constantius ruled there was no chance, and under a Catholic Emperor things righted themselves without the very violent methods proposed by the Sardican Fathers. Who were these men who attributed such arbitrary and unprecedented powers to the Papacy ? The president of the council was the most revered bishop of Christendom, the venerable Hosius, who had played a leading part (probably as president) at the Council of Nicæa. The chief personage in rank, as well as in fame, was Athanasius himself. The bishops were from West and East, from Italy, Gaul, Africa, Sardinia, and Spain ; from Dacia, Thrace, Macedonia, and Greece ; from Asia Minor, Crete, Egypt, Palestine, and Arabia.[2] The orthodox of every part of the Roman world were represented, and it is for this reason that I have dwelt upon the subject.

Next we have to defend St. Jerome from the accusation brought against him by Bishop Gore, that " what he recognised in Rome is recognised rather in the way of personal predilection than of ecclesiastical doctrine." Dr. Gore admits that the language of his letters to Pope Damasus " seems clear enough."

" But apparently later in life, after he had abandoned Rome in disgust, he can adopt exactly the opposite

after condemnation by the bishops of the region, himself appeal and take refuge with the bishop of Rome, let the latter write to the bishops of the neighbouring province to examine and decide the matter. And if the condemned bishop desires the Pope to send a priest *a latere*, this may be done. And if the Pope shall decide to send judges to sit with the bishops, having authority from him who sent them, it shall be as he wills. But if he thinks that the bishops alone suffice, it shall be as his wisdom shall think fit.

[1] Dr. Gore thinks the canons do not recognise an existing or essential right, but confer a privilege, and I admit that there is some truth in this—they give a new extension to an acknowledged right. But Dr. Gore's reason is a bad one. He builds, not on an examination of what was the practice and theory up to that time, but simply on the words of the third canon : " If it please you, let us honour the memory of B. Peter the Apostle." " If it please you " is a regular formula ; obviously

it implies that the canon need not be passed, and that its form may be altered, but not necessarily that it contains a novelty, for the same formula may be used to introduce a definition of faith. The reference to St. Peter is simply an honorific mention of the ground of that primacy of the Pope which is being so remarkably utilised against the Arians. No doubt a new honour would have been paid to St. Peter even by a canon which merely sanctioned the existing custom of appeals to Rome, which the Eusebians had evaded, and (as far as they dared) even denied.

[2] See full list of countries in Athan. *Apol.*, 36.

tone. 'The custom of the Roman Church,' he says in effect, 'has no more authority than the custom of any other Church. The episcopate at Rome has no more authority than any other episcopate.' 'If it is a question of authority, the world is greater than the city. Wherever there is a bishop, at Rome, or at Eugubium, or at Constantinople, or at Rhegium, or at Alexandria, or at Tanis, he has the same worth (*meritum*), the same priesthood (*sacerdotium*). The power of wealth or the humility of poverty do not make a bishop higher or lower. They are all successors of the Apostles.' This passage is not quoted by Roman controversialists, for a very plain reason, because it indicates that the authority of the Roman see rested for Jerome on what is variable in a theologian—on sentiment, on expedience, on feeling—not on what is invariable, the basis of doctrinal authority."

It is really painful to meet this passage once more in the ninth edition of Dr. Gore's work. Apparently he does not live and learn. This same silly argument (I am sorry to use such an adjective, but one must sometimes say what one thinks) was elaborated also in Dr. Gore's *The Church and the Ministry*, but he did not invent it, and it has been over and over again exposed, though Dr. Gore chose and chooses to ignore the remarks of "Roman controversialists," and to declare *in nine editions* that they still refuse to deal with the subject. I pointed out in the *Dublin Review* for January, 1898, that a reply to this same objection was to be found in so old a book as Archbishop Kenrick's *Vindication of the Catholic Church* (Baltimore, 1855), in Stone, *The Invitation Heeded* (1870), and in Dr. Ryder's admirable *Catholic Controversy* (1886), a book which Dr. Gore had no right to overlook, if he was venturing on the same ground. All these works are prior to Dr. Gore's first edition of *Roman Catholic Claims*. But this particular point was answered both by Dr. Rivington and by Father Richardson. I dealt with it at length in the article I have just referred to, and I have no doubt at all that Dr. Gore would be unable to reply to the exposition there given. I will hastily summarise it here.

St. Jerome objects to the Roman custom which gave a place of honour, even sometimes above priests, to the regionary deacons, who were functionaries of great secular importance. Much as he loved Rome, he had no idea that every Roman custom was necessarily right, nor does any Catholic to-day think so. He appeals to the world from the city. A priest, according to St. Jerome's well-known theory, was in Apostolic times the same as a bishop, and a bishop has the same *sacerdotium* "bishopship," whether he is pope, patriarch, or what not. Hence (the argument is rather strained) one might as well put a deacon above a bishop, a patriarch, or a pope at once, as above a simple priest, for all share in the same order of priesthood. Who doubts that St. Jerome is right in saying that the bishop of Gubbio is as much a bishop as his metropolitan, the bishop of Rome, and that the bishop of Tanis is as much a bishop as his patriarch, the bishop of Alexandria? And who does not see that this very argument implies that they differ in jurisdiction, while they are equal in bishopship? It is inconceivable to me how Dr. Gore (and many other Protestant controversialists) can dare to attribute to a father of the fourth century the doctrine that all bishops have equal jurisdiction, and that metropolitans and patriarchs have no more authority than their suffragans. If St. Jerome had really argued that the bishop of Tanis was not subject to the bishop of Alexandria, he would have been contradicting the Council of Nicæa, which confirmed the patriarchal rights of Alexandria and Antioch! But enough of this singularly ill-judged attack on St. Jerome's consistency. I will only add that it seems to me that the letter in question does not belong to his later life, but that it is a very early one.[1]

We can now hear St. Jerome's famous words in his letters to Pope Damasus, without imagining that they express mere "personal predilection," or that he afterwards changed his mind :—

"I ought to consult the chair of Peter and the faith praised by the mouth of the Apostle, asking now the food of my soul, where of old I received the garment of Christ in baptism. Away with envy, away with all canvassing of the Roman power : it is but with the successor of the fisherman and the disciple of the cross that I speak. Following no one as chief but Christ, I am in communion with your blessedness, that is, with the chair of Peter. On that rock I know the Church was built. Whosoever shall eat the lamb outside that house is profane. If any be not with Noe in the ark, he shall perish beneath the sway of the deluge. . . . Vitalis I know not, Meletius I reject. I know not Paulinus. Whoso gathereth not with thee, scattereth. . . . Define, I beseech you, if it pleases you, and I will not fear to speak of three hypostases. If you bid, let a new creed be established after the Nicene, and let us who are

orthodox confess our faith side by side with the Arians in similar words. But the whole literary faculty uses hypostasis in the sense of *ousia.* . . . Are we to be separated from Arius by walls, but united in heresy? . . . Far be this from the faith of Rome ; may the religious hearts of the people drink no such impiety! Let three hypostases be no more mentioned, if you please, and let one be held. . . . Or if you think fit that we should say three hypostases, we do not refuse. But believe me, there is a poison beneath the honey" (*Ep.* xv.). "On the one side storm the raging Arians, supported by the powers of the world. On the other a Church torn in three parts (Antioch) tries to seize me. Meantime I cry aloud : If any is joined to the chair of Peter, he is mine ! Meletius, Vitalis, and Paulinus all say that they adhere to you. If one of them asserted it, I could believe him ; but now either two of them or all three are lying," etc. (*Ep.* xvi.).

Dr. Gore has a last refuge. St. Jerome cannot have meant what he said ! "One cannot fail to catch the tone of exaggeration, almost of irony, in the second of these passages." Is it conceivable that the irony was directed against St. Damasus, by a recluse who was really in a grave difficulty between the contending parties, who all declared that they were on the side of the Pope? Was Jerome likely to write with elaborate rudeness to his own bishop?

Nearly forty years later, St. Jerome wrote to the greatest heiress in the world who was entering upon religious life :—

"I had nearly left out what is most important. When you were a child, and Bishop Anastasius, of holy memory, ruled the Roman Church, a fierce storm of (Origenist) heretics from the East tried to sully and destroy the simplicity of faith which was praised by the mouth of the Apostle. But that man of richest poverty and Apostolic solicitude straightway

---

[1] My reason is this. The same doctrine, that deacons at Rome are above priests, is attributed to a certain Falcidius by Ambrosiaster (*quæstiones ex utroque mixtim*, 101, among St. Augustine's works, vol. iii., Appendix). This was probably under Damasus, or not much later. The book of Falcidius seems to have been new when Jerome wrote his letter on the subject. Consequently I attribute the letter to the time of Damasus (366-384) or not long after. St. Jerome died in 420.

smote the noxious head and stopped the mouth of the hissing hydra. And because I am afraid, nay, I have heard the rumour, that these poisonous shoots are still alive and vigorous in some, I feel that I ought, with the deepest affection, to give you this advice, to hold the faith of holy Innocent, who is the successor and son of that man, and of the Apostolic see, and not to receive any foreign doctrine, however prudent and clever you may think yourself to be" (*Ep.* 130, A.D. 414).

Here there is no irony, and St. Jerome is aged, and close to his end; yet he speaks of Anastasius and of Innocent in their relation to the faith just as he spoke to Damasus.

Let us turn to Augustine, for we cannot pass over the greatest of the theologians of the West, and that African Church to which Protestants have been so strangely fond of appealing.

We have heard this Doctor call the Roman see the rock against which the gates of hell do not prevail. Like Optatus before him, he uses a list of the Roman bishops as a witness against the Donatists.[1] He uses the same argument against the Manichæans.[2] He not only asks "Who is unaware that most blessed Peter is the first of the Apostles?"[3] but he tells us that this Primacy remained in the Roman Church.[4]

But his witness is yet more remarkable to the position of the

Pope as ultimate judge on matters of faith. The history of the condemnation of the Pelagian heresy throws a flood of light upon this question. I have not space even to summarise it here. But I will notice a few points.[5]

On hearing that Pelagius had been absolved by the Council of Diospolis in Palestine, the African Church met in two simultaneous councils at Carthage and at Milevis. Each of these councils thought it necessary to write to the Pope a letter asking him to approve their condemnation of the heresy.[6]

"This act, lord brother, we thought right to intimate to your holy charity that *to the statutes of our littleness might be added the authority of the Apostolic see* for the preservation of many and the correction of the perversity of some. We doubt not that your reverence . . . will make such a judgement that we shall all rejoice in the mercy of God," and so on.

A separate letter was sent by five bishops, St. Augustine, the friend of his conversion, St. Alypius, his disciple Evodius, his biographer St. Possidius, and the Primate, Aurelius :—

"We wish it to be approved by you whether our stream, though small, flows from the same head of water as your abundant river."[7]

Pope St. Innocent replied in the most "papal" style[8] that the councils had done well in preserving the customs of the Fathers, so as to refer to the Apostolic see, and he confirms their decisions. It is interesting to know what contemporaries thought of the tremendous claims made in these letters. St. Augustine says :—

---

[1] *Ep.* 53.

[2] "I am held in the communion of the Catholic Church by . . . and by the succession of bishops from the very chair of Peter, to whom the Lord, after His resurrection, commended His sheep to be fed, up to the present episcopate." *Contra Ep. Manich. Fundam,* 5. Compare: "the chair of the Roman Church, in which Peter sat, and in which Anastasius sits to-day" (*C. Litt. Petil.,* ii. 51).

[3] *In Joann.* 56.

[4] The Roman Church *in qua semper Apostolicæ Cathedræ viguit principatus"* (*Ep.* 43).

[5] I have dealt with the history in detail in two articles in the *Dublin Review,* Jan. and July, 1897.

[6] Aug., *Epp.* 175, 176.

[7] *Ep.* 177.

[8] Aug., *Epp.* 181–2.

" To all of these letters he answered in the manner which was the right and the duty of the bishop of the Apostolic see." " The letters of Pope Innocent by which all doubt about this matter was removed." " Let blessed Innocent also reply. . . . Do you see what the catholic faith holds by her minister ? "[1]

St. Prosper : " The rising pestilence was first cut short by Rome, the see of Peter, which, having become the head to the world of the pastoral office, holds by religion whatever it holds not by arms." " They fell, when Innocent of blessed memory struck the heads of the deadly error with the Apostolic sword," etc.[2]

Marius Mercator, disciple of Augustine : " Three councils were assembled. From thence relations were sent to Rome, together with the books. The Apostolic sentence in reply to the councils followed."[3]

Prædestinatus, a contemporary work : " Pope Innocent, when the matter was referred to him by nearly all the African bishops, wrote the condemnation of both Pelagius and Celestius. These latter, however, whether before they were condemned by the universal Church or after they were condemned, did not cease to write," etc.[4]

With these words of the ancients before us we are not at liberty to doubt the agreement of the Western Church as a whole with the claims of Innocent. Let St. Augustine speak once more :—

" Do you think these Fathers are to be despised (viz. Irenæus, Cyprian, Reticius, Hilary, Ambrose, whom he had been quoting) because they all belong to the Western Church, and I have mentioned no Eastern bishop among them? What are we to do, since they are Greeks and we are Latins? *I think that you ought to be satisfied with that part of the world in which our Lord willed to crown the first of His Apostles with a glorious martyrdom.* If you had been willing to hear Blessed Innocent, the president of that Church, you would have long ago disengaged your perilous youth from the snares of the Pelagians. For what could that holy man answer to the African councils except what from of old the Apostolic see and the Roman Church with all others perseveringly holds ? "[5]

On Sunday, September 23rd, 417, St. Augustine preached at Carthage against Pelagianism a famous sermon, which concludes with the most celebrated words to be found in his writings :—

" My brethren, be of one mind with me. Wheresoever you find such men do not hide them, have no perverse pity. Refute those who contradict and bring to us those who resist. For already two councils have been sent to the Apostolic see concerning this matter, *and rescripts have come from thence. The case is concluded:* would that the error would soon cease also. *Causa finita est, utinam aliquando finiatur error.*"[6]

The question of dogma was indeed decided, but the case was not concluded. While Augustine spoke, letters were on their way from a new Pope—for Innocent had lately died —declaring that Celestius and Pelagius were the victims of malicious calumny and had never taught the errors attributed to them.

Rome is rarely in a hurry, and the Eternal City has won many victories by delay. But, for an exception, there was now an impulsive, arbitrary, and hasty Pope, who committed a series of mistakes during the year and a half that he occupied the chair of Peter. We have mentioned the most serious of these. Celestius had handed in a profession of faith which ended thus :—

" What I have received from the fountain of the Prophets and Apostles

---

[1] *Ep.* 186 ; *c.* 2 *Epp. Pet.* ii. 3 (5); *Op. imperf.,* vi. 11.
[2] *De Ingratis,* i. 39 ; c. Collat., xxi.
[3] *Commonit. c. Pel.,* 11.
[4] *Hær.,* 88.

[5] *c. Jul.,* i. 13.
[6] *Serm.* 131, 10.

we offer to be approved by the judgement of your Apostleship, in order that, if by chance any error of ignorance has crept in upon us, being but men, it may be corrected by your decision." [1]

Pelagius similarly sent a profession, with a still stronger declaration of submission to the Pope :—

"This is the faith, most blessed Pope, which we have learned in the Catholic Church, which we have ever held and hold. If we have by chance set down aught in it unskilfully or without due caution, we desire to be corrected by you, who hold both the faith and the see of Peter. If, however, this confession of ours is approved by the judgement of your apostleship, then whosoever desires to blacken me, will prove, not that I am a heretic, but that he himself is unskilful, or not a Catholic." [2]

It was not unnatural that Pope Zosimus should be deceived by such humility. His letters to Africa, full of "papal claims," are at first gushing with the hope of absolving these repentant or calumniated sons, and then with anger at the incredulity of the Africans. [3] But he was

soon undeceived, and with startling suddenness published the final condemnation of the heretics whom he had been on the point of acquitting. St. Augustine had to write treatise after treatise to defend the Pope from the charge of contradicting himself. He shows that Zosimus always upheld the same doctrine, but that he was tricked by the two heretics into believing in their orthodoxy.

"Pelagius for a time seemed to say what was in accord with the Catholic faith, but he was *unable to deceive that see to the end.*" [4]

The Pope's decree was sent "to be carried throughout the Catholic world," [5] and appended to it were the original resolutions of the African councils. [6] It is always spoken of by St. Augustine as a final and irreformable judgement. The summary by St. Possidius in his life of St. Augustine gives in a succinct form the African view of the whole business :—

"And since these heretics were trying to bring the Apostolic see round to their view, African councils of holy bishops also did their best to persuade the holy Pope of the city (first the venerable Innocent, and afterwards his successor Zosimus) that this heresy was to be abhorred and condemned by Catholic faith. *And these bishops of*

---

[1] *Ap. Aug. de Pecc. Orig.*, xxiii. 26.

[2] In Appendix to vol. x. of St. Augustine. That saint makes a similar profession in the dedication of his work, *Contra duas Epistolas Pelagianorum*, to Pope St. Boniface. After speaking of the Pope's "higher seat," "loftier pinnacle," etc., he says : "This reply, then, I have decided to send to your holiness, not that you may learn from it, but that you may examine it, and wheresoever anything may chance to displease you, correct it."

[3] A memorial against the Pelagians was addressed to Pope Zosimus by Paulinus, a deacon of Milan, a disciple of St. Ambrose, and his biographer. Its testimony to the supremacy of Rome in matters of faith is most remarkable. I will quote but the commencement : "I beseech justice of your blessedness, Lord Zosimus, venerable Pope. The true faith is never disturbed, *and above all in the Apostolic Church*, in which teachers of false faith are as truly punished as they are easily discovered, that they may die in the evils they have committed, unless they correct them, so that in

them may be that true faith which the Apostles taught, and which the Roman Church holds together with all the doctors of the Catholic faith. And if, like the other heresiarchs (who, *long since judged by the Apostolic see, or by the Fathers,* and expelled from the bosom of the Catholic Church, are given over to eternal death), these also, who are or shall be discovered, remain in their perfidy, *let them be delivered to the spiritual sword to be destroyed,*" etc.

[4] *De Pecc. Orig.*, xxi. 24.

[5] *Ibid.*

[6] This was generous of Zosimus, since relations between Africa and Rome were strained also by the affair of Apiarius about this time ; on this point, see my article, "Apiarius," in *Dublin Review*, July, 1901.

so great a see successively branded them, and cut them off from the members of the Church, giving letters to the African Churches in the West, and to the Churches of the East, and declared that they were to be anathematised and avoided by all Catholics. The judgement pronounced upon them *by the Catholic Church of God* was heard and followed also by the most pious Emperor Honorius, who condemned them by his laws, and ordered them to be treated as heretics. Wherefore many of them have returned to the bosom of holy Mother Church, whence they had wandered, and are yet returning, as the truth of the right faith becomes known against this detestable error." [1]

Nothing could be clearer here than the inferiority of the 120 bishops of the African councils to the decisions of the Popes. Nor does St. Possidius doubt that it was right (such was the view of those days) to punish by civil laws those who would not obey the see of Rome. No less than nineteen bishops were deposed by the Pope and banished by the Emperor for refusing to sign the papal decree. Against the chief of these, Julian, St. Augustine wrote a work in six books, and he was engaged on the sixth book of a second reply when he died, twelve years after the decree. [2]

---

[1] *Vita Aug.*, xviii.

[2] It is very noticeable that this heretic himself did not dare openly to refuse the authority of the Pope. He, like Pelagius and Celestius, sent a profession of faith to Rome, in which he said :—

" We have written and sent this to your holiness, as it appears to us according to the Catholic rule. If you think we ought to hold otherwise, write us a reply. But if it is impossible to contradict us, and yet some wish to stir up scandal against us, we declare to your holiness that we appeal to a plenary council " (in Appendix to vol. x. of St. Augustine). Thus he does not venture to appeal from the Pope to a plenary council, but only to enforce the Pope's hypothetical approval of his doctrine ! St. Augustine puts down the

These notes on the condemnation of the Pelagians may be supplemented with a quotation from the celebrated appendix to the letter of St. Celestine to the bishops of Gaul, sent a few years after St. Augustine's death by the hands of St. Prosper :—

"Since many who boast the Catholic name remain in the condemned opinions of heretics, whether by wickedness or by want of wisdom, and presume to dispute with pious champions of the faith, and since, while they do not hesitate to anathematise Pelagius and Celestius, yet they reproach our doctors with exceeding the right measure, and *because they profess to follow and approve only what the most sacred see of the most blessed Apostle Peter has sanctioned and taught against the enemies of the grace of God by the ministry of its prelates,* it has become needful to inquire diligently *what the rulers of the Roman Church have judged concerning the heresy* which arose in their time, and what they decided to be held against the dangerous defenders of free will. At the same time we shall add *some decisions of African councils, which the Apostolic prelates, in fact, made their own when they approved them.* Therefore, in order that they who doubt as to any point may be instructed, we make *the institutions of the holy Fathers* plain in a compendious table, so that any who is not over-contentious may recognise that the whole dispute is summed up in the short quotations subjoined, and that *no reason for contradiction remains for him, if he believes and confesses with Catholics.*" [3]

The words are probably St. Prosper's. It would be difficult to express more clearly the final and

demand to a desire of notoriety (*C. duas Epp. Pel.*, iv. 12 (34)). Julian goes on to explain that his reason for not signing the Pope's letter is his unwillingness to condemn the innocent unheard, as though he accepted the doctrine, which of course he did not.

[3] Celestine, *Ep.* xxi., and in Appendix to St. Aug., vol. x.

binding nature of what the writer lower down calls "The inviolable sanctions of the most blessed Apostolic see."[1]

NOTE.—On p. 118 Bishop Gore refers in a note to the treatise de Aleatoribus, commonly printed with St. Cyprian's work. The literature on this subject within recent years has reached an enormous amount. (It will be found chronicled in Ehrhard, Bardenhewer, or Harnack.) The net result is that it is practically certain that the author is either a Novatian or a Donatist, consequently the witness is of less interest. It appears that he was an anti-pope belonging to one of these two sects (see Harnack, Chronol., ii. p. 379), so that Dr. Gore's remarks lose all their point.

CHAPTER VII

THE DEVELOPMENT OF THE PAPACY IN LATIN CHRISTIANITY

AT the outset of this chapter Dr. Gore poses the difference between his view of history and the Catholic view in the clearest manner. The Papacy is "a natural development of circumstances, and it is in the fashioning of circumstances that we look for the hand of Providence." The Catholic historian declares that it is a *supernatural development of circumstances.* Dr. Gore's preceding phrase is not ambiguous: "It is one of those historic growths which indicate a divine purpose latent in the tendencies of things and the circumstances of the world." To a Catholic, on the other hand, the Papacy seems a "great historic growth" which cries aloud to the world of the direct and mira-

[1] It is sometimes thought that the so-called semi-Pelagians of Southern Gaul, to whom this appeal is addressed, included no less a person than St. Vincent of Lerins, and that he was one of those who found difficulty (and no wonder) in some of the harsher expressions in St. Augustine's writings, while professing "to follow only what the most sacred see of the most blessed Apostle Peter has taught." It is interesting to find the same "ultramontane" doctrine openly professed in St. Vincent's Commonitorium. His words about Pope Stephen already referred to are exceeded by the conclusion of his whole work. As a crucial instance of his doctrine, he takes the recent Council of Ephesus, and shows how in it writings earlier than Nestorius were examined for the proof of the faith. But he has yet another and, it is implied, a still higher authority to cite in his last chapter of all: "Though all this would suffice and more than suffice for the destruction and extinction of every profane novelty, yet that nothing may be wanting to such a fulness, in the last place we add two authorities of the Apostolic see, one of holy Pope Sixtus, who now venerably illustrates the Roman Church; the other of his predecessor, Pope Celestine of blessed memory, which we have also thought necessary to add here" (c. 32). He then quotes some words of Sixtus against novelty, and comments "omnino apostolice," and then cites the very letter of Pope Celestine, from the appendix to which I have been quoting above. He adds that if anyone denies his doctrine "he must first insult the memory of Saint Celestine . . . then deride the definitions of holy Sixtus . . . and also the statutes of blessed Cyril . . . and the synod of Ephesus besides, that is to say, he must trample on the judgements of the holy bishops of nearly the whole East. . . . Lastly, the whole universal Church of Christ, with its teachers the Apostles and prophets . . . unless he is willing to violate the Apostolic definitions and ecclesiastical decrees by which . . . all heretics . . . have been condemned."

St. Vincent of Lerins, the great supporter of "antiquity," evidently holds that obedience to the definitions of the holy see is a tradition from antiquity!

culous action of God. Its growth, its vigour, its influence, are a part, and an essential part, of that visible unity of the Body of Christ which He has set in the world as the great witness to Himself.

It is a poor fisherman put to death, an ignominious death, in the circus of Nero, while a companion of his, as a Roman citizen, is beheaded on the Ostian Way. Less than three hundred years pass, and the successor of the fisherman is at the head of a religion which stretches beyond the limits of the Roman world. " It is they," cries St. Leo in one of his sermons on St. Peter and St. Paul, " who have promoted thee, Rome, to this glory, that, a holy nation, an elect people, a city of priests and kings, made the head of the world by the sacred see of blessed Peter, thou mightest have a wider rule by divine religion than by earthly domination. For although, increased by many victories, thou hast carried the rights of thy empire over sea and land, yet less is what the labour of war has won thee than what has been subdued beneath thy sway by Christian peace " (*Serm.* 72).

No sooner has the master of the world become Christian than he moves, in obedience to the divine plan, yet all in ignorance, the secular capital away from the see of Peter to the banks of the Bosphorus, and never again is Rome the permanent residence of the Court. Thus the independence of the head of the Church from imperial influence is secured. If we wish to know how necessary to Christendom this was, we have but to glance at the line of the bishops of Constantinople—orthodox when an orthodox emperor had made them, heretics when the emperor was a heretic; and in almost all cases, from Eusebius of Nicomedia till Photius and beyond, time-servers and slaves to the civil power.

When the Eastern Emperor can no longer control the destinies of Europe, and the young nations of the West are strong in their new Christianity, another system is devised by Him who rules men to His own ends. The Pope becomes independent of the Emperor, and a sovereign among the kings of the West. Rome is the nursing mother of the Western nations, and to her they owe much of their law as well as all their faith. The mediæval world has passed away now, and the Pope's little kingdom has passed with it, and we yet await the means which God will take to ensure the independence of His Vicar in the coming ages. The wonderful lessons of the past tell us that we can trust in the future for a succession of those victories and sufferings, losses and triumphs, which have made the history of the Papacy of such varied and absorbing interest.

Now, Bishop Gore has well summarised on pages 107–108 a part of the circumstances of the development of the papal influence and its beneficial effects. He has pointed out how in early times " Rome in her dignified repose was the recipient of appeal after appeal from the East," how "the orthodoxy of Rome was conspicuous throughout all the controversies on the Trinity and the Incarnation," how " the tendency of events in the secular world was running steadily in the direction of her exaltation." The question remains whether all this is " natural development " or whether it is not a marvellous manifestation of divine power. I cannot sketch the history here ; I can only remind the reader that some of the greatest of Protestant writers and thinkers have been unable to speak of the course of the story of Rome without a kind of awe and wonder at something beyond what they meet in other fields of historical research.[1]

But one point at least I can and will establish against Dr. Gore. I will show that the recourse of the Easterns to the Papacy was not simply "because it was undisturbed by the Oriental heresies," but because its peace was looked upon by the Easterns themselves as the result of the promise of Christ to St. Peter. In the last chapter the evidence of the Western Church as to the Roman Catholic claims was carried as far as the early part of the fourth century, but the last Eastern evidence mentioned was from the Council of Sardica in 343, though incidentally the witness of the historians Socrates and Sozomen was referred to. It will be in place here to deal with some samples of the Eastern witness on the same subject.

But in the first place it is necessary to point out a slight divergence

---

[1] Bishop Gore admits, "There is, then, in the deepest sense of the words, a providential purpose in the Papacy; and it is impossible to estimate all that the Church as a whole owes to Rome." But he does not really mean "in the deepest possible sense." He puts on the same level "a divine vocation given to the Eastern Church as the great mother of theology, at least as conspicuous as that which was entrusted to the West in the sphere of discipline and government." Perhaps; but at least very far less conspicuous than the divine vocation given to the West, and Rome in particular, of picking up the East repeatedly out of the mire of heresy! Still less conspicuous than the divine vocation given to Rome of being an inerrant and permanent centre of unity! "It does not follow because governmental authority or centralisation was the one thing needed in the seventh century that it is the one thing needed now." I should not for an instant admit that these were the only things needed in the seventh century. But I can hardly believe that Dr. Gore does not admit their necessity in the Church of England as a prelude to any other possible reforms.

between the ways in which East and West looked at the see of Peter.

In the East it became the rule that ecclesiastical divisions should coincide with the civil divisions of the Empire. In the West the claim of a city to metropolitan rank rested usually on the claim that it had been the first in the region to receive Christianity.

(a) Consequently the Eastern Fathers would say, "Rome was the imperial city, so that St. Peter naturally made it the capital of the new world-wide Faith. He also gave a second and a third place in the Church to Alexandria and Antioch, as being the second and third cities of the empire." This view is perfectly correct, but it allows of being stated in the form, "Rome has the first place as being the capital," and this form admits of a wrong meaning, for St. Peter's action in the matter is not expressed.

(β) The Western Fathers see three Petrine sees, of which one has inherited all St. Peter's primacy, while the other two have a reflection of it. The Westerns are willing to go on to moralise on the suitability of the great capital, the modern Babylon, to be the Jerusalem of the second covenant, but this is a secondary consideration.

In themselves the two doctrines are one; but the points of view are different, and their divergence became apparent when Constantine moved the capital to Byzantium. It did not strike the Easterns as possible to move to Constantinople the primacy left by Peter to Rome; but to a large number of them it seemed obvious that the new metropolis of the world must have a patriarchate, and must rank above Alexandria and Antioch. By the time that the Arian troubles were clearing up, the bishop of Constantinople had already arrived at a position of great power.

The first attempt to get this existing authority regularised was made in the Council of Constantinople in 381, which for its creed was later counted as œcumenical. The third canon runs thus : " The bishop of Constantinople shall hold the first rank after the bishop of Rome, because Constantinople is new Rome." There is no mention of patriarchal jurisdiction over Thrace and the ancient autonomous exarchates of Ephesus and Cæsarea. The consent of Alexandria could hardly be expected ; that of the distracted Antioch was unimportant. It was probably expected that Rome would have no objection.

But the Pope had no care to please the Emperor or the Court bishop. In the following year St. Damasus held a great council at Rome, in which it seems that the creed of Constantinople was accepted. But the canons were not confirmed, and against the third canon in particular an imposing protest was made. It runs thus :—

"Although the Catholic Churches diffused throughout the world are one bridal chamber of Christ, yet the holy Roman Church has been preferred to all other Churches, not by any synodical decrees, but has obtained the primacy by the voice of our Lord and Saviour in the Gospel, saying : 'Thou art Peter, and upon this rock I will build My Church, and the gates of hell shall not prevail against it ; and I will give to thee the keys of the kingdom of heaven, and whatsoever thou shalt bind on earth shall be bound in heaven . . .' There was also added the fellowship of the blessed Apostle Paul, who not at another time (as the heretics do vainly babble) but striving under Nero Cæsar, on the selfsame day was crowned together with Peter with a glorious death in the city of Rome ; and together (*pariter*) they consecrated the above-said holy Roman Church to Christ the Lord, and set it above all cities of the world

by their glorious presence and venerable triumph.

" Therefore the first see of Peter the Apostle is that of the Roman Church, not having spot or wrinkle or any such thing.

"And the second see was consecrated at Alexandria in the name of blessed Peter, by Mark, his disciple and evangelist. And he himself being sent by Peter the Apostle into Egypt, preached the word of truth, and consummated a glorious martyrdom.

" The third see of the most blessed Apostle Peter is had in honour in Antioch, because he dwelt there before he came to Rome, and there first arose the name of Christians for the new people.[1]

There is nothing here with which the Easterns would have disagreed. But they would have urged with some reason, that the disposition with regard to Alexandria and Antioch, which was universally attributed to St. Peter, would have been altered by the Apostle had he lived in the fourth century!

A new attempt to get recognition for the Court see was made seventy years later. The circumstances were extraordinarily favourable. The patriarch of Alexandria had just been convicted of heresy and violence, and had been ignominiously deposed. The patriarch of Antioch, Domnus, had been deposed the year before by the Robber-Council, and was now allowed only lay communion. His successor was in a doubtful position, and was not strong enough to refuse the cession of the three provinces of Palestine to make a patriarchate for Jerusalem. He was glad to retain the favour of Constantinople at the price of losing one place in rank.

[1] This will be found in the collections of Councils under Gelasius, but it is restored to Damasus by C. H. Turner (*Journal of Theol. Studies*, i., July, p. 560), following Thiel, Friedrich, Hefele (*Councils*, vol. 4, pp. 43–5, Eng. tr.), Maassen, Zahn, etc.

Many must have desired the humiliation of Alexandria.[1] The new bishop of the imperial city, Anatolius, was a courtier, who meant to retain the good will of both Emperor and Pope.

Consequently, in the fifteenth session of the great council of Chalcedon, after the retirement for the day of the papal legates and imperial commissioners, under the presidency of Anatolius, the famous 28th Canon was passed by a large number of the bishops, the rest having departed. It confirms the Canon of 381, and adds:—

"For to the see of elder Rome, because that was the seat of empire, the Fathers have very properly rendered the first honours (οἱ πατέρες εἰκότως ἀποδεδώκασι τὰ πρεσβεῖα), and moved by the same consideration, the most venerable 150 bishops accorded equal honours to the most holy see of new Rome, reasonably judging that the city which is the seat of the Empire and of the Senate, and which enjoys the same honour as the old queen, Rome, should in ecclesiastical matters be magnified like her, being second after her."

The canon goes on to regularise the already existing patriarchate of Constantinople. The opening remark was evidently intended as a compliment to Rome, with the intention of pleasing St. Leo.[2] There

was every reason to expect the Pope's approval, for in the first session of the council, Paschasinus, the papal legate and president of the council, had actually granted to Anatolius the first place after the papal legates.

But the day after the passing of the canon the legates made their protest against the informality of proceedings in which they had refused to join. As Paschasinus had clearly put his foot in it before (for the Pope's instructions were clear that the Nicene arrangement was to be respected), his colleague Lucentius assumed the office of reserving the matter to the Pope, though the Imperial Commissioners had given their assent to the decision of so large a body.

The synod could not but respect this protest. The council was now over, and they had only to conclude by sending to the Pope the Acts and an enclosing letter. In this letter the Fathers of the council tell St. Leo that it is he who has saved the Faith, " being constituted to all

[1] The excesses of Dioscorus were before the eyes of all. The teaching of St. Cyril was under a cloud. The persecution of St. Chrysostom by Theophilus was not forgotten, and had redounded as much to the glory of Constantinople as to the discredit of Alexandria. And Constantinople had a new glory in the orthodoxy and martyrdom of Flavian the year before.

[2] Dr. Gore says, on the contrary: "Nothing can be more certain than that the bishops that enacted this canon did not regard the privileges of Rome as a part of the divine and essential constitution of the Church or they could not have used the expression 'the Fathers gave': nothing can be more plain than that the primacy of Rome is in their eyes a 'primacy of

honour.'" But they did *not* use the expression "the Fathers gave"! I suppose that Dr. Gore has been misled by Hefele (*Hist. of Councils*, iii. p 412, Eng. trans.). The Greek *cannot possibly* mean this. Ἀποδίδωμι does not mean "I give a present," but "I return a loan," or "I render a due." St. Leo found no fault with the expression, nor did he ever suggest that anything had been implied which was derogatory to the dignity of the Roman Church. That the Fathers of Chalcedon did not regard the Roman primacy as a mere primacy of honour will be seen later (pp. 91–2). That they regarded it as founded by St. Peter appears repeatedly from their own words. There is nothing to object to in the words, "To the see of elder Rome, because that was the seat of empire, the fathers have very properly rendered the first honours." The first place was not "given" by "the Fathers," but by St. Peter, and "the Fathers" continued to "render" the same honour which Peter had "given" to the capital.

the interpreter of Blessed Peter." All had been in concord, and Christ had been with them, and Leo by his legates had presided as a head over the members. Dioscorus had trampled down the Vine of the Lord like a wild beast (Ps. lxxix. 14), and "in addition to all his other crimes had extended his madness against him who had been entrusted with the guardianship of the Vine by the Saviour, that is, against your holiness." Notice here that (1) St. Leo is the official interpreter of the confession of Peter (according to his own assertion, and the repeated acclamations of the council), and (2) that the reference to the "guardianship of the Vine" given to him "by the Saviour" is a still more distinct statement that the Pope's power is derived from the original grant to Peter. There is no doubt that the Fathers of Chalcedon would have allowed all that St. Damasus had claimed. They had no idea that their doctrine of the coincidence of ecclesiastical with secular jurisdiction could be in any way contrary to the prerogatives of Rome as "the Apostolic see," and they thought that St. Peter himself, in fixing his primacy in the capital, had given the precedent for their view that Constantinople ought now to rank in the second place.[1]

Further on in the letter the canon itself comes in for consideration. The Fathers point out that, in conceding a patriarchate, it is merely approving what has long been customary. As for the question of rank, the "Apostolic ray" has often beamed as far as Constantinople, so that they hope Leo will confirm it. If the legates had resisted it, and had reserved it to the Pope, that was no doubt because they wished the benefit of this disciplinary enactment as well as that of the faith to be attributed to Leo himself! As his sons have joined themselves to their head, so he will confirm their decisions and give pleasure to the Emperor. Soon afterwards the Emperor and Anatolius both wrote to ask the Pope to accept the canon, the confirmation of which had been expressly reserved to him.[2]

The replies of St. Leo are in his gravest and most fatherly style.[3] He speaks of the dangers of ambition, and points out that Anatolius should have been satisfied with the generosity shown by the Apostolic see in passing over the irregularity of his election. He does not see anything in the canon inconsistent with the respect due to Rome, but he insists upon the principle that the rank of the great sees is from Peter, and not from their secular importance, and that he has no right to alter the arrangements confirmed at Nicæa.

The answer of Anatolius is abject.[4] He had instantly obeyed, he says, all the Pope's injunctions; the canon was not his work—the blame is to be laid on the clergy of Constantinople! "But even so the whole force and confirmation of the acts

[1] It is true that the legate Lucentius had complained of an insult to the Apostolic see, but he did not mean by this anything in the wording of the canon, but that it had been passed after the retirement of the legates from the session of the council, and in spite of their refusal to countenance the discussion of the proposal. It is certain that St. Leo saw in the canon nothing in any way reflecting upon the unique dignity that he himself claimed with so much assurance. This point was noticed by a writer in the *Dublin Review*, January, 1903. But the reason he suggests for St. Leo's view is founded on the mistranslation of ἀποδεδώκασι by "gave."

[2] *Ep. Leon.* 100, 101.
[3] To the Emperor Marcian (*Ep.* 103), to the Empress Pulcheria (*Ep.* 105), and to Anatolius himself (*Ep.* 106).
[4] *Ep. Leon.* 132.

was reserved to your holiness." The result of this was that the canon was not copied into the Western collections, nor is it in the Arabic version. But naturally the course of things at Constantinople went on as before, for the system had been long in exercise.

We have now seen the divergence between East and West in regard to the point of view from which they regarded the privileges of the see of Rome. I wish now to give only two crucial instances to show both in theory and practice how the Easterns treated the Popes. These shall be the condemnation of Nestorius by the Council of Ephesus, and the deposition of Dioscorus by the Council of Chalcedon. I choose these instances, first, because these councils represented the whole East, and give a far more general view than can be afforded by a few patristic quotations, and secondly, because Bishop Gore regards these councils as œcumenical, and will have, in consequence, the more re-regard for the means by which they arrived at their decisions, and for the opinions of the bishops who composed them.

Nestorius became bishop of Constantinople in the winter of 427-8. In 429 his heretical teaching was sufficiently spread to induce St. Cyril, patriarch of Alexandria, to preach against him. Nestorius tried to gain the Pope to his side in two letters, but received no reply, for the Pope had been asking information from St. Cyril. The latter wrote to Pope Celestine, that the evil had reached a climax, and he now felt bound to denounce it, since ancient customs of the Churches recommended him to communicate the matter to the Pope, who must now signify his view to the bishops of Macedonia and to all the bishops of the East. Celestine at once held a

council at Rome.[1] He then writes to Cyril, August 11th, 430 :—

"Joining to yourself, therefore, the sovereignty of our see, and assuming our place with authority, you will execute this sentence with accurate rigour: that within ten days, counted from the day of your notice, he shall condemn his false teachings in a written confession," etc., (otherwise he is cut off from our body) (Mansi, iv. 1020).

John, patriarch of Antioch, urged Nestorius to yield, although the ten days was a somewhat brief delay. Cyril held a synod in order to draw up a suitable formula of the faith, and then sent the papal notification to Nestorius in a letter calculated to wound and exasperate rather than conciliate.[2] Nestorius refused to submit, and appealed to the council which both he and the orthodox Easterns desired to see assembled; for the whole Antiochian school of theologians, though not heretical, was dissatisfied with the definitions of the Alexandrian patriarch. Theodosius II. issued a letter convening a synod at Ephesus for Pentecost, and wrote also a bitter letter to Cyril, insisting that he above all must be present.

St. Cyril now wrote to the Pope to ask an important question; the letter is lost, but the Pope's answer has preserved the inquiry :—

"You ask whether the holy synod ought to receive a man who condemns what it preaches, *or because the time of delay has elapsed, whether the sentence already delivered is in force*" (Mansi, iv. 1292).

The question was whether the synod might judge once more one

[1] Councils hastily formed, or meeting at regular intervals, were the Pope's advisers, like the "congregations" of to-day. The other great sees held similar councils from time to time.

[2] Mansi, iv. 1069: "Your uncouth and distorted teachings," St. Cyril says.

who had been already condemned by the Pope. St. Cyril was, of course, anxious that the question should not any longer be considered open, but that Nestorius should be treated as a condemned criminal. One would have thought he might have anticipated that if the Pope approved of the meeting of a council, and sent legates to be present at it, it was a matter of course that he intended Nestorius to be granted a fresh trial, and a full examination to be made. But this did not suit St. Cyril at all. He took up the ground that what the Pope had settled could not be revised except by special permission from the Pope himself.

St. Cyril, as the first bishop of the world after the bishop of Rome, assumed the presidency of the council, and insisted upon opening it on June 22nd, 431, in spite of the demand of sixty-eight bishops, and of the imperial count, that the arrival of John of Antioch should be awaited. Cyril believed that the delay of that patriarch was intentional; it was inexplicable that the papal legates had not come; and with 160 bishops he decided (with good reason, even though some may think it would have been yet better to delay) that proceedings must commence.

It does not appear that Celestine had commissioned Cyril to be his representative at Ephesus. But in the absence of any letter from the Pope, the Alexandrian bishop considered that the excommunication he had published as papal delegate against Nestorius was still in force, and that he appeared as its author at the council, to see it approved and rectified, but not reconsidered. This is evidently the reason why he has regularly designated himself at the beginning of the acts of each session of the council as "Cyril of Alexandria, who also held the place of the most sacred and holy archbishop of the Roman Church, Celestine."

Nestorius refused to appear. The definitions submitted to him by St. Cyril were approved, and the correspondence between Rome, Alexandria, and Constantinople was read, and many testimonies of earlier writers were cited against the doctrine of Nestorius. Thus the doctrine both of Cyril and of Nestorius was freely examined. But before evening the synod proceeded to the signature of the sentence of deposition. Hefele oddly remarks : "The intermediate speeches are not known to us." But it is evident that there were no intermediate speeches, for the acts up till this point are very full, and sufficient to occupy a sitting of enormous length. It is clear that Cyril did not propose any discussion of the sentence of deposition. In his view it was not to be revised by the Council, which had completed its duty when it had examined the theological question. He allowed his own writings to be examined, but the papal sentence was simply to be accepted. The following is the form proposed. It was signed by all the bishops, who by evening numbered 198, without any remarks being added by any of them.

"The Holy Synod said : 'Since the most impious Nestorius will not obey our citation,[1] and has not received the most holy and God-fearing bishops whom we sent to him, we have necessarily betaken ourselves to the examination of his impieties; and having apprehended from his letters, and from his writings, and from his recent sayings in this metropolis, which have been reported, that his opinions and

[1] If Nestorius had consented to appear, he would of course have been allowed to defend himself.

teachings are impious, *we being necessarily compelled thereto by the canons and by the letter of our most holy father and colleague, Celestine, bishop of the Roman Church*, with many tears, have arrived at the following sentence against him :—

"'Our Lord Jesus Christ, Who has been blasphemed by him, defines by this present most holy synod that the same Nestorius is deprived of episcopal dignity and of all sacerdotal intercourse.'" (Mansi, iv. 1212.)

They were compelled by the canons—for they had cited Nestorius three times, and judgement went against him by default. They were compelled by the letter of Pope Celestine—that is, by his former letter to St. Cyril, for no other had yet come—since no permission had been sent for revision of the sentence which St. Cyril had issued.

The legates of the Pope, who had suffered from storms at sea, at last arrived, and the second session of the council was held on July 10th. The bishops Arcadius and Projectus were representatives of the Roman council of the Pope, and the priest Philip was his personal representative. The latter announced that Celestine had long since decided the matter by his letter to Cyril, and had now sent a new letter. This was read in Latin and Greek. [1] It contained an exhortation to the synod, and the names of the legates who were to carry into effect what Celestine had before decided. The Pope doubts not that the synod will assent. This letter was received with acclamation. Projectus calls attention to the mandate given to the legates. Firmus, bishop of Cæsarea, explains that the synod had in fact already executed the sentence according to the rule laid down by the former letters of the Apostolic and Holy See. Arcadius

[1] Mansi, iv. 1284.

apologised for the late arrival of the legates on account of bad weather. Philip then thanked the council for the applause by which the bishops had joined themselves as holy members to their holy head, for they were not ignorant that Peter is the head of the faith and even of all the Apostles. He asks for information as to the acts of the first day, that the legates might confirm them. (Mansi, iv. 1289.)

To these acts of the second session is appended the letter of Celestine to Cyril, containing the answer to his question. The Pope replies that God does not desire the death of a sinner, but that He desires all men to be saved; so that Nestorius is, as we should have expected, to have a fresh chance. But *the letter had arrived too late*, and the permission was anyhow made useless by the refusal of Nestorius to appear.

In the third session, on the following day, the legates said they had read the acts, and approved them. But in order that they might give a confirmation, the formula of deposition must be read again. This was done on the motion of Memnon, bishop of Ephesus, (it seems that Cyril had not yet arrived in the hall). Then each of the three legates pronounced a solemn confirmation in the name of the Pope. The introduction of the speech of Philip is famous (*Ibid*, 1296) :—

"It is doubtful to no one, nay—it is known to all ages, that holy and blessed Peter, the prince and head of the Apostles, the pillar of the faith, and the foundation of the Catholic Church, received from our Lord Jesus Christ, the Saviour of the human race, the Keys of the Kingdom, and that to him was given the power of loosing and binding sins, who up to this time and always lives in his successors and gives judgement. His successor, therefore, and representative, our holy and most blessed

Pope, bishop Celestine, has sent us to this synod to supply his place," etc.

At the request of Cyril, who was now present, the legates added their signatures to those of the bishops who had signed the deposition.

It is not necessary to comment either upon the claims made by Philip or upon the statement made by the council that they were "obliged" by the letters of St. Celestine, or upon St. Cyril's original execution of the Pope's orders. In all these points we see that the Pope is indeed the head; he deposes the bishop of Constantinople, he is of greater authority than the council.

Of the Council of Chalcedon something has already been said, and I have now to deal with a single point only, the deposition of Dioscorus. In this case he had not been previously condemned by the Pope, but his sentence was expressly left to the council. He was summoned three times by the council, as Nestorius had been. After his third refusal to appear, the papal legate Paschasinus, president of the council, repeatedly asked the opinion of the Fathers, and all agreed that he was to be condemned. Then Julian, bishop of Hypæpa, moved that, since Dioscorus as president of the Robber-Synod of the preceding year had given an unjust judgement, so now he should be judged by Paschasinus, who held the authority of Blessed Leo, and by the holy council. "*We therefore urge your sanctity, who hold—or rather you* (in plural) *who hold the place of the most holy Archbishop Leo*, to pronounce sentence against Dioscorus, and to define concerning him what is in the canons. For we all, and the whole œcumenical council, are of one mind with your sanctity."

Paschasinus said once more: "Again I say, what is the pleasure of your blessedness?" Maximus, Bishop of great Antioch, said: "With what your sanctity thinks, we agree."

Then Paschasinus, with his fellow-legates, Lucentius and Boniface, "holding the place of the most holy and blessed Patriarch of Great Rome and Archbishop, Leo," solemnly recited a summary of the crimes of the bishop of Alexandria, and concluded:—

"Wherefore the most holy and most blessed archbishop of great and elder Rome, by us and the present most holy synod, together with the thrice-blessed and praiseworthy Peter the Apostle, who is the rock and base of the Catholic Church, and the foundation of the orthodox faith, has stripped him of the episcopal and of all sacerdotal dignity; wherefore this most holy and great synod will vote what is in accordance with the canons against the aforesaid Dioscorus" (Mansi, vi. 1048).

After this each bishop gives his adhesion to the sentence in a few words. I give the first of these little speeches—that of Anatolius of Constantinople—as an example:—

"Anatolius, bishop of royal Constantinople, new Rome, said: 'Agreeing in all things with the Apostolic see, I vote with it as to the condemnation of Dioscorus, who was bishop of the great city of Alexandria, who had proved himself unworthy of all sacerdotal office, by disobeying in all things the canons of the Fathers, and by not choosing to obey, when thrice canonically summoned.'"

At the end of these speeches we find the words, "And when all the holy bishops had spoken, they signed as follows." The signatures were 294 in number. To what were they appended? *Without doubt to the condemnation pronounced in the name of the synod, and at its request by Paschasinus*, and possibly also to the reports of the little speeches of confirmation just delivered. It cannot be denied that the Chalcedonian Fathers, like those of Ephesus, amply recognise the right of the Pope to condemn one of the great patriarchs.

We may now take up a challenge of Dr. Gore's: "I believe indeed that *none of the Greek Fathers of the first six centuries connects the position of the bishop of Rome with the promise to St. Peter*" (p. 91). In a note he admits that a universal statement is somewhat hazardous.

Now it is true that the great Greek commentators (and the early Latin commentators too), in annotating Matthew xvi. and John xxi., do not make any reference to the successors of St. Peter;[1] they simply speak of his own primacy. Why on earth should they do more? As a rule, it is only the popes themselves who directly cite these passages as the grounds of their own jurisdiction. It was right for them to show that it was on spiritual authority, and not on the influence of wealth or prestige, or on the support of the Emperor that they leaned. But even in the East, where a more worldly view was taken, as we have seen, Rome is regularly spoken of as "the Apostolic see," although there were plenty of Churches in the East which had an Apostolic origin, and the bishops of Antioch and Alexandria considered themselves in a sense successors of Peter. But when St. Chrysostom at Antioch calls his bishop "another Peter," he explains that Antioch had to give up the Apostle to Rome.[2] The expression "the Apostolic see" is especially significant in the mouth of an Athanasius and a Cyril, for they were bishops of the second Petrine

see. If this is not a connexion "of the position of Rome with the promise to Peter," I do not know what is; for we have seen how much authority these two saints attributed to the Pope.

We have heard the connexion openly expressed at the Council of Sardica: "The head, that is to say, the see of Peter." "Let us honour the memory of Blessed Peter the Apostle" (above, p. 75). This is before the middle of the fourth century. In 431 we have the constant use of "the Apostolic see" by the Fathers at Ephesus, their acclamations of the letters of Celestine, and their acceptance of the claims of Philip. In 451 we have the letter of the Council of Chalcedon to St. Leo (p. 87 above) with its definite reference to Leo being the interpreter of Peter, its statement that he was entrusted with the guardianship of the Vine "by the Saviour." We have also the famous acclamations of the Fathers: "It was Peter who spoke thus through Leo!"[3] In the same year we have the letter of Theodoret (p. 60).

Later on the evidence is more abundant. I will instance the bishops of Dardania in 494: "We who desire to serve the Apostolic see without blame, *according to the divine precepts* and the statutes of the Fathers."[4] This is clear enough. A certain bishop Flavian (?) of Rhodope wrote to the heretical Peter Fullo, bishop of Antioch, about 479: "But you have been canonically sifted by our prelates, that is, by the prince of the Apostles, Peter, to whom the Lord said: "Whatso-

[1] I suppose that mediæval and even modern commentators do not always speak of this extension of the text, or rather deduction from it.
[2] *Hom. in Inscr. Act*, ii. 6.

[3] Mansi, vi. 972. Compare the cries of greeting of the Oriental bishops to Peter, bishop of Corinth, when he went over to the other side of the council and sat with them, thus taking the orthodox side: "Peter agrees with Peter! Welcome, orthodox bishop" (Mansi, vi. 681).
[4] Mansi, viii. 13.

ever thou shalt bind," etc., with reference to a Roman synod, apparently one held by Pope Simplicius.[1] In 512 many Eastern bishops wrote to Pope Symmachus : " Even as the blessed Prince of the glorious Apostles taught, whose chair Christ, the best of Shepherds, has entrusted to your beatitude." " Hasten to help the East from which the Saviour sent the two great lights of day, Peter and Paul, to you to illumine the whole world. . . ."[2] A few years later the Archimandrites and monks of Syria secunda write to Pope Hormisdas : " To the most holy and blessed patriarch of the whole world, Hormisdas. . . . Since Christ our God has made you *the chief of shepherds* and teacher and physician of souls, it is proper for us to unfold the sufferings which have come upon us, and to point out the merciless wolves who are scattering the sheep of Christ. . . . To you is given the power of binding and loosing. . . . Look upon Peter, that prince of the Apostles, whose see you adorn, and Paul who is the vessel of election, who have illuminated the world. . . ."[3] In 515 the Emperor Anastasius writes to the Pope to ask him to compose a trouble in Scythia : " We are inquiring what our God and Saviour taught the holy Apostles in His divine words, and especially blessed Peter, in whom He constituted the firmness of His Church."[4] To the same Pope, Dorotheus, bishop of Thessalonica writes : " I write to the blessed head of your holiness, signifying that we rejoice together with the blessed see of most holy Peter, that it is governed by such a hand," etc.[5] John, bishop of Constantinople, is induced to sign the famous "formula of Hormisdas" in 516,[6] which was

required by this Pope of a great many bishops, and again frequently by later Popes. It was eventually, in an enlarged form, approved by the eighth œcumenical council.

The patriarch declares in his letter to Pope Hormisdas that he rejects all the heretics whom the Pope rejects, and that the see of Peter and the see of the imperial city are one and the same, by which he means to say that their union is complete. The formula prefixes to the anathematizations of heretics the following introduction :—

" It is the first condition of salvation to keep the rule of right faith and in no degree to deviate from the tradition of the Fathers, for the sentence of our Lord Jesus Christ cannot be passed over, which says : ' Thou art Peter, and upon this rock I will build My church.' *These spoken words are proved by their effects*, because in the Apostolic see religion is always kept undefiled. Therefore, desiring not to fall from this faith, and following what has been constituted by the Fathers in all things, we anathematise," etc. Later on : " Wherefore, in all things following the Apostolic see, as we have said, we also preach all that has been decreed by it, and therefore hope to be in one communion with you, which the Apostolic see enjoins, in which is the true and perfect solidity of the Christian religion, promising that in future those who are separated from the communion of the Catholic Church—that is to say, those who do not consent to the Apostolic see—shall not have their names recited in the holy diptychs."

The difficulty in getting such a formula signed was not in the least due to its extolling the Apostolic see, as some Anglican controversialists seem to think (for no objections were ever raised on this score), but to the explicit way in which the promise was exacted that not only should all the heretics be condemned, and the teaching of Rome followed, but that none of the dead

---

[1] Mansi, vii. 1119. [2] *Ibid.*, viii. 221.
[3] *Ibid.*, viii. 425. [4] *Ibid.*, viii. 384.
[5] *Ibid.*, 386. [6] *Ibid.*, 451.

who had been cut off from communion by Rome should be mentioned in the liturgy. The wording of the formula was not intended to exalt Rome, but to exclude all the evasions of the half-orthodox, who had been so long in schism through the arbitrary acts of the Emperors Zeno and lately, Anastasius.

It seems hardly necessary to continue the list. From the earliest times appeals from the East to Rome had been common, but the letters sent are mostly lost, and it was not necessary that every one should contain a reference to St. Peter. In the sixth century more are preserved, and within only a few years many more could be quoted; e.g. the Emperor Justinian : "The primacy of the Apostolic see"; "Let your Apostleship show that you are indeed the successor of Peter the Apostle."[1] His statements (contained in his code) that the Pope is the "head of all the holy Churches," "the head of all the holy bishops of God,"[2] and how he saw this carried out in practice, are well known. I will not, however, add more, except to refer to another patriarch of Constantinople, Epiphanius, in 520 :—

"It is my custom (or prayer?) greatly to unite myself with you, and to embrace the divine dogmas which have been handed down to your holy see by the blessed and holy disciples and Apostles of God, especially of the chief of the Apostles, Peter, and to think nothing more precious."[3]

The reader can, if he thinks fit, refer also to the explicit application to the Pope by Stephen, bishop of Larissa, of John xxi. 17, in 521,[4] to the multiple evidence in the long Acts of the Council of Constantinople under Mennas in 536,[5] but

the witness becomes too frequent to be pursued further. I have only referred to it because of Bishop Gore's challenge; it would have been more effective as controversy to have followed out the actual exercise of the papal prerogatives, or even the statement of them in words, rather than the mere reference to St. Peter.

But as I have been dealing with a challenge, I will not omit one other point. Dr. Gore has written :—

"Allnatt, in his *Cathedra Petri*, can at least be trusted to accumulate all the legitimate references to the Fathers in support of a papal view—indeed, he does not often stop here—but under the heading 'St. Peter lives and teaches in his successors' and 'rules in his own see' he cannot quote a single Father of the first four centuries, except one Pope, Siricius (A.D. 386)."

The remains of Fathers of the first four centuries are rather limited in extent, and the mystical idea of Peter in his successors is not at all a natural way of expressing the authority of the Apostolic see. In the third edition of Mr. Allnatt's careful work (1882) I cannot find this heading, so I suppose it was inserted in a later edition. But I will give what I have myself observed. Besides Siricius I find:—

2. The Council of Arles, 314, to St. Sylvester: "(Rome) where the Apostles daily sit (as judges)." This is a remarkable saying of this great and early council of the whole West.

3. The letter of Pope Julius to the Eusebians (342) quoted by St. Athanasius : "What we have received from the blessed Apostle Peter, that I make known to you."

But the fifth century is not to be despised. Dr. Gore is aware that the series of genuine decretal letters of the popes begins only with Siricius, at the end of the fourth century, and before that we have little but

[1] Mansi, viii. 515, 516. These letters are before he was emperor.
[2] *Ibid.*, viii. 795.   [3] *Ibid.*, viii. 502.
[4] *Ibid.*, viii. 741 foll. ; cp. 748.
[5] *Ibid.*, 874 foll.

gments of their writings. Some btestant controversialists object to dence drawn from the writings of pes, as if all of them, saints or t, were unscrupulous boasters, d as if (which is ridiculous) they bitually asserted what nobody ceived. But, on the contrary, to Catholic, and therefore to one eking to find the truth, the evi- nce of the claims made by the opes themselves has obviously a ery special value. Now, I find his reference to the voice or assist- nce of Peter particularly common n the letters of the popes, for it is a modest way of asserting their authority without attributing any- thing to their own person.

4. St. Innocent, 417 : " I think that, as often as a question of faith is dis- cussed, all our brothers and fellow- bishops should refer to none other than to Peter, the author of their name and office " (In St. Aug., *Ep.* 182).

5. St. Zosimus, 418 : " For (Peter) himself has care over all the Churches, and above all of that in which he sat, nor does he suffer any of its privileges or decisions to be shaken," etc. (*Ep.*12).

6. St. Boniface, *c.* 420, to his legate Rufus : " B. Peter looks upon thee with his eyes " (*Ep.* 5).

7. Philip, legate of Celestine at Ephesus, 431 : " Who even until now and always lives and judges in his suc- cessors " (above, p. 90).

6. St. Sixtus III., *c.* 435 : "B. Peter in his successors has delivered what he received " (*Ep.* 6).

7. St. Leo, frequently : " Who does not cease to preside in his see, who will doubt that he rules in every part of the world ? " (*Serm.* 5, etc.).

I have added half a century to Dr. Gore's four. Let us hear the Westerns echo the Popes :—

8. Pelagius the heretic, 418 : " You who hold both faith and the seat of Peter " (above, p. 80).

9. St. Peter Chrysologus, Doctor of the Church, bishop of Ravenna, 450 : " Blessed Peter, who lives and presides

in his own see, gives the truth of the faith to those who seek " (Letter to Eutyches, *Ep.* 25, *inter Leon.*).

And the Eastern Church :—

10. Theodoret, 451, to Pope Leo : " This thrice blessed pair (Peter and Paul) rose in the East, and sent forth their rays everywhere, but it is in the West that they have had their glorious setting, and *from thence they illumi- nate all the world*" (*Ep.* 113 and Leo, *Ep.* 52).

11. St. Pulcheria, Empress, 451, to St. Leo (*Ep.* 77) : " The Apostolic confession of your letter."

12. Council of Chalcedon, 451 : " It is Peter who has spoken this by Leo " (above, p. 92).

I daresay these might easily be added to ; I subjoin two as ex- amples of the sixth century, both from the East :—

13. Eastern bishops to Pope Sym- machus, 512 : " You who are daily taught by your sacred teacher Peter to feed the sheep of Christ entrusted to you throughout the whole habitable world " (Mansi, viii. 221).[1]

14. Two bishops of Thessaly to Pope Boniface II. in 521 : " For these things we appeal to your Blessedness and the Apostolic see, and through it we be- lieve we hear and adore thrice blessed Peter, and the chief Shepherd of the Church, Christ our Lord " (Mansi, viii. 748).

I have only given these quota- tions to show how misleading are Bishop Gore's general statements. The idea that Peter speaks and rules in his successors is, of course, not to be taken literally. It means that his authority endures in them, and also that his prayers give them especial assistance.

We must now turn to an un- pleasant subject — forgeries and frauds. Dr. Gore begins by saying

[1] See letter of Juliana Anicia, daughter of the Emperor of the West, Flavius Anicius Olybrius : " The vicars of glorious Peter the Apostle." This is the lady for whom the Vienna MS. of Dioscorides was written (Mansi, viii. 496).

that Saint Leo was a real saint, but that he was "unscrupulous," "strangely blinded in conscience," because "he quoted as a canon of Nicæa what had been shown to demonstration to be a canon of Sardica and not of Nicæa" (pp. 110, 111). Who had shown it to be a canon of Sardica, and when? Dr. Gore is a little out in his facts, as well as quite unique in his theory of what a "real saint" is![1] Then there are the famous Forged Decretals, which Dr. Gore—in contradiction to all the best Protestant historians—declares "represent a step of immense importance in the aggrandisement of the papal claim."[2] If I were to treat Dr. Gore as he treats St. Leo, I should assume that he knows better, but is "strangely blinded in conscience" and "unscrupulous," when papal claims are in question. But of course I am perfectly sure that Dr. Gore is in "invincible ignorance," and I cannot but find his contention amusing. Will he kindly ask himself: *If it had not already been firmly established that a papal decretal was an absolute law for the Church, what would have been the use of forging any at all? and what could any forgeries add to this absolute sway?*[3]

[1] Mr. C. H. Turner (*Journal of Theol. Studies*, April, 1902, p. 390) does not think St. Leo was a liar. See esp. pp. 393–5.

[2] Supposing it certain (which it is not) that St. Leo and his advisers knew or remembered the letter of an African council twenty years earlier, which showed that the canon in question was not in the Eastern collections of Nicene canons, it is not unnatural that the Pope should suppose the manuscript in his archives was more complete. If the Africans had known the canon was Sardican, they would have accepted it, but they knew nothing of that synod.

[3] The Isidorian decretals were not made in Rome, but in Germany; not in favour of the popes but in favour of bishops, that the latter might be free to appeal to Rome, and not be subject to secular tyranny. The later papal laws on the subject were at-

"Nay, even *conscious* fraud is familiar element in official acts the Roman see" (p. 111). On one example of this "familiar" phenomenon is given! It is the omission in the sixteenth century in the breviary lessons for June 28th the name of Pope Honorius from the list of heretics condemned by the sixth œcumenical council. But the removal of what might easily be misunderstood and what was certainly disedifying in a prayer-book was hardly a "fraud"! "The love of interpolations and falsification is alive still among Roman controversialists. The interpolations in St. Cyprian are still printed as an integral part of the text by Father Hurter and quoted by Allnatt." *Both of these writers give elaborate notes on the words*, explaining the evidence for their antiquity, which they rather undervalue.[4] They leave their authenticity doubtful. Is this fraud? I should accuse Dr. Gore himself of want of charity

tributed by the forger to the first three centuries, in order to ensure that new popes would respect these ancient customs and enforce them, and that they would be obeyed. There was no idea of enlarging the papal power, nor was it enlarged, though centralisation was increased.

[4] The famous interpolated passage in St. Cyprian, *De Ecclesiæ Catholicæ unitate*, 4, consists (as found in printed editions) of a conflation of the original text with an alternative form which had been substituted for it not later than about 350. The alternative form *was not intended in favour of Rome*, but embodies the usual argument against the Novatians or the Donatists. The reasons I gave two years ago for attributing it to St. Cyprian himself have appeared conclusive to Harnack, Hans von Soden, and many other scholars. The most remarkable part of the "interpolation" lies in the words: "*He who deserts the Chair of Peter upon whom the Church was founded, is he confident that he is in the Church?*" This is the recognised teaching of Optatus and Augustine, but it is equally clearly the view of Cyprian (above, ch. v.). My articles appeared in *Revue Bénédictine*, July and October,

in his accusation, did I not know that it is not incompatible with the recognition of both writers as even "real saints"!

"The certainty that Ultramontane writers will always be found manipulating facts and making out a case," p. 113. Nothing would be easier than for me to bring the same accusation against Dr. Gore, were it not that I know his personal character. Does he know of any "Ultramontane writer" so unscrupulous, unfair, untruthful, as "Janus"? Has he met with any "Roman controversialist" as disreputable as Dr. Littledale? I

often disagree with arguments put forward on the Catholic side, nay, they often annoy me greatly. There is no subject on which argument does not lead people to exaggerate. But Protestant history from the Magdeburg centuriators and Foxe to Froude, has been a series of lies, whether intentional, careless, or prejudiced. There is nothing like this on the Catholic side, since the Middle Ages. I do not make Dr. Gore answerable for Protestant historians, nor will I myself be answerable for mediæval forgers, who, however, seldom worked in favour of the Papacy.

CHAPTER VIII

THE NATURE OF SCHISM

I F we believe in the unity of the Church Militant, there is no necessity for a chapter devoted to the elucidation of a mysterious question: "What is schism?" Evidently schism is a cutting off from the unity of the Church. The Church is as it were an organism. Cut off a branch from the tree, the branch withers; amputate a member from

1902, and January, 1903. Another article (*Journal of Theol. Studies*, Oct., 1902) is necessary to the argument, which depends largely on the history of the MSS.

With regard to Pope Honorius, I think personally that he was quite rightly condemned by three general councils and a whole succession of popes. But I cannot agree with Bishop Gore that the Sixth General Council in condemning him shows that it had "no, even rudimentary, idea of the papal infallibility" (p. 104). On the contrary, I am sure that the acts of the council prove it to have held strongly the inerrancy of the Apostolic see, in spite of the (apparently well-meant) mistake of Honorius. But I am treating of this matter elsewhere.

the body, that member dies. These are the metaphors used by the Fathers; they found them suggested by the New Testament, and they applied them unanimously and consistently.

But Bishop Gore does not believe that the Church is one. These plain expressions are of no use to him. He cannot refer to the Fathers for a definition. He is in great difficulties to find one for himself. "If $\sigma\chi\iota\sigma\mu\alpha$ does not mean a cutting off from unity, what *can* it mean?" This is the question he has been obliged to pose to himself, and no wonder it takes him a whole chapter to answer it, no wonder that when one has read the chapter, one is uncertain whether he has given an answer or not.

"Schism does not merely mean breaking away from the episcopal form of government" (p. 125). Why should it? (And on what ground does Bishop Gore think it necessary to adhere to an episcopal form of government? It is not stated in the Bible to be necessary. An order of ἐπίσκοποι is mentioned, but so are deaconesses and widows.)

On page 126 two definitions are attempted : " Schism, considered apart from heresy, as a sin excluding from the benefits of Church life, means *wilful self-withdrawal from the legitimate succession of the Catholic Church* on the part of an individual or party, or, in a secondary sense, the *wilful causing of a breach inside the Church.*" The italics are Bishop Gore's.

Here we have two kinds of schism. The former of the two definitions is useless, for it begs the question. How am I to know what is "the legitimate succession"? I cannot find that Dr. Gore ever gives a plain reply. On pages 126, 127 Dr. Gore discusses the kinds of "temper" which lead to schism. On page 128 he quotes five great saints of the early Church to the effect that there is no graver sin than schism. We know what they meant by schism —the cutting off from unity. But what Dr. Gore means he has not yet explained. Then we have a comparison on pages 128, 129 between Donatism and Anglicanism. I admit that the resemblance is not great (in fact I have pointed this out above, ch. iii.), except in the fact of both being cut off from unity— separated from the Catholic Church throughout the world. Next we come to an example of the second (improper) kind of schism, " the wilful causing of a breach inside the Church." The instance given is the ordination of Paulinus as patriarch of Antioch by Lucifer of Cagliari, a subject on which Father Puller has written voluminously and paradoxically. So far as I can see, Dr. Gore is perfectly right in thinking that

the zeal of Lucif... of ... his discretion in this cas... ...nly ... ...ad no canonical justificat... ... the orthodox party had lo... ...is... ...ithout a bishop. Meletius ...he ...made bishop of Antioch, ...of ... Arian auspices, and his o... ...ne ...s of his orthodoxy did no... ...ie ... the original vice of his ... ...ut ...ent. The orthodox party n... ...ly ...cog-nised his right nor tru... ...r- ...pro-fessions, but it was in... ... ...ity. The two holy bishops, P... ...e ...nd Meletius, ruled side by ... ...s ...he same city over a divided fl... ...ch looked upon the other ... ...n-truder. Rome and Alexa... ...at is, the whole of the West, ...e hundred sees of Egypt,—c ... ...t it otherwise, St. Athanasius, ...-tagonist of the Catholics, and thodox West—held to Paulin... without ever declaring St. M... and his people to be cut off from Church, for they were orthodox, a were supported roughly by whole East, that is by the patriarchate of Antioch and Asia Minor, and championed by St. Basil. An arrangement was proposed that on the death of either of the rivals the survivor should remain sole bishop. But party spirit in Antioch ran too high, and when St. Meletius died he was succeeded by the Flavian whom Chrysostom has made so famous. The disappointment was enough to make St. Gregory Nazianzen resign the see of Constantinople. Yet even now neither the West nor Egypt excommunicated Flavian, who appeared to have put himself in the wrong, and after the death of Paulinus's successor Evagrius, the actual communion of Rome was no longer denied to Flavian.

The interest of the position is this ; the rival bishops excommunicated one another, yet the one was believed by the East to be in the right (or rather, to be less in the

THE NATURE OF SCHISM 99

wrong), and the other by the West and Egypt, while East and West and Egypt were in full communion with one another.[1]

Contrast this with a similarly divided Church at Rome. Novatian was consecrated bishop in 251 in opposition to the legitimate Pope Cornelius. In the city he is supported by the confessors in prison, and in the first few months the whole world is divided on account of the schism at Rome. If anyone held with the wrong bishop of Rome, it was recognised that he was outside the Church. To hold with the wrong bishop of Antioch was a comparatively unimportant matter. St. Basil was not out of communion with Rome, because he thought St. Damasus had been misled in determining to give his preference to Paulinus.

Two Spanish bishops, who had been deposed or had resigned, induced Pope Stephen to decide that they should be restored to their sees. Their successors sought sympathy and assistance from St. Cyprian, who, with a council, examined the matter, and concluded (rightly or wrongly) that Stephen

had been deceived, and that on this ground his decision need not be obeyed. Suppose the rival bishops in the Spanish town were each recognised by a different set of Catholic bishops, it might happen that this "schism in the Church" might endure without either faction being cut off from unity. Strictly speaking, it would not be a schism.

The great schism of the West exhibits a more curious state of things. We find rival popes, followed by different kingdoms, and the uncertainty is so great that even now it has not been defined as a matter of faith which succession was the true one, though of course the Italian one is almost unanimously accepted. But there were saints on both sides. It was not a clear case, as that of Cornelius was against Novatian, and those who in good faith supported the wrong Pope could not be considered to be in schism, and the faithful of different countries, though on different sides, were not out of communion with one another.

But these are extraordinary and most unusual exceptions. The schism at Antioch is not used by Bishop Gore, as it is by Father Puller, as a parallel to the Church of England, and rightly, for there is no parallel at all. Both bishops were in communion with Catholics, and thus in communion with the whole world, and even, one may say, "mediately" with one another. Neither was excommunicated by Rome. But England, alas! cut herself off, and was cut off, from the whole world.

But Dr. Gore actually tries to show that the separation of England and Rome is only a "secondary" schism of the same character, though not altogether parallel, with that between the two bishops of

---

[1] Dr. Gore quotes Tillemont to the effect that, as two saints of the end of the fifth century, Elias and Flavian, had always remained in communion with Acacius by continuing in communion with Constantinople, Pope Hormisdas did his best to procure their exclusion from the diptychs, but that the Roman Church had to give way, and "do violence to her maxims" (pp. 130, 131). Rather "and understand the case better." If Elias and Flavian had not actually communicated directly with Acacius in wilful disobedience to the Holy See, the principles of the very strict Hormisdas would not demand their exclusion. The great Gallican writer, while a most sure guide in most matters, is fond of little hits at Rome which are often unjustifiable. I wish Dr. Gore would follow him in his general principles, and not in his occasional eccentricities, for Tillemont is a real and edifying Catholic in his history.

THE NATURE OF SCHISM

Antioch. He thinks the *temper of schism* worked on both sides, but on neither side was there that "withdrawal from the Church Catholic" which constitutes schism in the primary sense (p. 132).

Now "secondary schism" in Dr. Gore's sense is like a cut in a piece of cloth—the cut edges have been separated, but they remain joined to the rest of the piece of cloth. A "primary" schism—a schism in the ordinary sense, the full sense of the word—is like a cut right through the piece, so that there are two pieces.

In the case of the division between Rome and England there is a cut right through. If this is not a real, a complete cut, σχίσμα, I ask what is. How is it possible to cut more completely than to cut right through, and leave not a thread of connexion?[1]

Next the schism of East and West is alleged. "We make a grievous mistake if we suppose that it was the result of any single fact—like the claim of Rome or the *Filioque* clause." No indeed, for every schism is sure to invent a heresy to justify its existence, as St. Augustine tells us, and the denial of the claims of Rome and the refusal to accept the *Filioque* were mere excuses made by the Greeks to justify what was already in progress. The real cause of the schism is obvious. So long as the Pope was even nominally a subject of the empire, the emperors recognised him in theory (and whenever they were orthodox, in practice also) to be the ruler of the Church. But when he became independent, his influence with the emperors waned, and division gradually began. One can hardly tell when

[1] On pp. 133-4 Bp. Gore again refers to Victor and to Stephen, on whom see ch. v. and vi.

it became complete and final; perhaps we may say not till the fall of Constantinople in 1453.

"There is no Catholic principle which can justify us in supposing that either the Roman, the Eastern, or the Anglican Church has been guilty of the sin of schism, in that sense in which schism is the act of self-withdrawal from the Church Catholic" (p. 137).

I can only understand this to mean that Dr. Gore will not admit any principle to be Catholic which can justify us in supposing these things, for the ancient principle that schism is a breach of unity is as certainly Catholic as it is self-evident from the primary meaning of the word.

Lastly Dr. Gore lays down three propositions:—

1. "There is no such thing as an absolute authority in the Church." I do not know what this means, unless it means that there is no authority from which we cannot appeal to another, existent or imaginary (such, I mean, as an actually impossible council, or a consent of divided bodies). This will mean that nobody need obey anybody, unless he happens to agree. Dr. Gore thinks even the apostles were not infallible or absolutely to be obeyed, and that in matters of faith. He proves this by quoting a passage where St. Paul declares that *from his teaching there is no appeal!* It is almost incredible, so I give Dr. Gore's words:—

"The authority of a pope is not even on his own showing greater than that of an apostle, yet at the last resort St. Paul conceives of an appeal behind even his own apostolic authority. 'Though we, or an angel from heaven preach unto you any other gospel *than that which we preached unto you,* let him be anathema.'"

The italics are mine. There is no appeal from Paul to an angel from heaven, or to Paul himself "better instructed"—from Philip drunk to Philip sober.

We saw on Dr. Gore's first page that he was distrustful of logic. I have not thought it necessary to point out how consistent he has been in this throughout his work. But this paragraph seems to me the culminating point. If even an apostle is not infallible, are we to believe the New Testament? If no authority is absolute, is any to be obeyed?

"The papal authority," he continues, "could never be absolute, without appeal beyond it, unless it was indeed strictly infallible" (p. 138). True, so far as faith and morals are concerned; with regard to these the Pope's authority is absolute, and he is infallible. But his authority in government is absolute, yet he is not infallible; he may make mistakes in politics, in justice, in judgement, but he is to be obeyed. The same is the case in all human laws. There is no appeal from a British jury in criminal matters, yet a jury is not infallible, neither is the House of Lords so in civil cases, neither is the King, if his prerogative is brought in. But "absolute authority" there must be in human matters, even if mistakes are made, even if the innocent have to suffer, or else we have anarchy.

2. "There is no evidence of any divinely appointed order among bishops." I have given plenty of evidence to show that the primacy of the bishop of Rome was always looked upon by the ancient Fathers as of divine right, being that which was conferred on St. Peter by Christ Himself. "Of course, further than this, whatever claim Rome might have made as the Head of a united Christendom, is enormously weakened in force by the existence of millions of the Oriental Church separated from her communion, largely, perhaps we should say mainly, on account of the exaggeration of her claim to empire over other churches" (pp. 138, 139). So is the claim of Christianity enormously weakened by the millions of Chinese who do not accept it. So is the boast by the English Church of "comprehensiveness" weakened by the millions of East and West who regard her with horror largely, perhaps we should say mainly, on account of this boast. No doubt, if the Roman Church gave up her claims, there is no reason why she should differ from the Easterns, why she should not be as comprehensive as the Anglicans. Nor would there be any reason left, so far as I can see, why anyone should wish to belong to her or to join her.

3. Dr. Gore finally "recognises the force of the objection" that at least "the ancient Church knew no *permanent* breaches of communion within her body, and did not contemplate such as possible." The objection has very little force for Dr. Gore to acknowledge. No Catholic would formulate such a plea, nor would anyone who has any knowledge of the patristic period. The real objection has been stated above in chapter ii. The ancient Church denied that any breach of unity was justifiable, and declared that all who, in any way, for any reason, were wilfully cut off from unity, were outside the way of salvation. The ancient Church not only did not contemplate breaches "within" her body as possible, but regarded visible unity as the first and paramount necessity of the Church, the necessary condition of true faith, and of the participation of the graces of Christian fellowship.

CHAPTER IX

ANGLICAN ORDINATIONS

DR. GORE wrote his chapter on Anglican ordinations before the Bull of Leo XIII. had condemned them as invalid. He has not rewritten it since, and much of it calls for no reply. To the Bull itself he has devoted three pages in a supplementary chapter (pp. 200-2), and I am obliged to say a few words on this point, though I should have preferred to leave it alone. One feels as if one were committing a piece of personal rudeness, when one is obliged to tell one who believes himself to be a priest that from the standpoint of Catholic theology his claim must be denied. And pain is certainly caused without much good being done.[1]

Against Leo XIII. Dr. Gore's first point is this :—

"Anglican Orders are repudiated, because there was not in the Edwardine service for ordaining priests explicit mention, in the words of ordination, of the office of priesthood to which ordination was being conferred, *and* more precisely of 'the power of consecrating and offering the true body and blood of the Lord,' *i.e.* in the Eucharistic sacrifice" (p. 200).

I have italicised the word *and*— it should be *or*. The name of the priesthood *or* the mention of its grace would either of them be sufficient. Consequently Dr. Gore's next statement is mistaken.

"But it is manifest, from the existing services of ordination, that the specification of this function of the priesthood is equally absent, not only from the Coptic rite, but also from the ancient Roman rite for ordination to the priesthood in the third century, and later down to the ninth century."

But the ancient Roman form makes special mention of the Dignitas *Presbyterii* and of the *secunda Dignitas*, which has the same meaning. So does the Coptic office mention the priesthood.[2]

---

[1] Even Dr. Gore shows signs of almost irritation when he deals with this question. Newman's preface to Hutton's book is said to be "surely very unworthy of its great author." "Canon Estcourt argues in a manner unworthy of him in his miserable chapter vi." "It is, indeed, a matter more for profound regret than for surprise that Mr. Hutton, of the Oratory, who objected some years ago to the evidence for Anglican Orders, found himself shortly afterwards unable to accept the evidence for the Christian Religion." If this means anything it means that the evidence for the validity of Anglican Orders is as strong as that for the truth of Christianity (p. 148 note, p. 151 note, and p. 146).

[2] The Abyssinian form, and also the newly discovered form attributed to Sarapion of Thmuis, are the only ancient forms which can be said to lack definiteness. In neither case is it certain that our information is complete, and the date of both is doubtful. They contain no mention of sacrifice, and the name of priest is unaccountably omitted. I say "unaccountably," because in the forms for the diaconate and episcopate the name of the office is expressed. In the form for the presbyterate there is only the mention of the elders appointed to assist Moses. These were as regularly compared with priests as the Levites were with the deacons, and the reference is retained in the Anglican ordinal. Perhaps this mystical comparison may be sufficiently definite to make the forms valid as they stand. A comparison of the Coptic form suggests that part of the commencement of the prayer, where the word priesthood occurred, has been accidentally omitted in the two doubtful forms. The parallel forms for the episcopate and diaconate add probability to this conjecture.

"Confessedly the English Church desired to return to the richer and fuller conception of the function of the priest which had prevailed in primitive times, before the function of offering sacrifice had assumed the undue prominence given to it in the Middle Ages."

It is hardly possible not to think that again Dr. Gore is writing hastily. We know that the reformers, whether English or German or Swiss, had the habit of appealing to earlier times in favour of their novel views. Of course they declared (absurdly, as Dr. Gore will agree) that the Eucharistic sacrifice was not a part of the teaching of the primitive Church. But the alterations in the ordinal and in the "communion service" were obviously not directly motived by the desire to return to more primitive conceptions, but by the determination to eliminate all trace of sacrifice in the new Book of Common Prayer. A comparison of the "Mass" in the first Prayer Book of Edward VI. with the Sarum Missal will show that every single reference to sacrifice has been omitted. The Anglican ordinal exhibits the same phenomenon. In neither case is there the smallest indication of any attempt to conform to what might have been, even in those days, supposed to be primitive. These are plain facts, which do not brook denial. It is well to look them in the face, however unpleasant they may be.

"'Be' thou a faithful dispenser of the word of God and of His holy Sacraments' includes, no doubt, the commission to celebrate the Eucharistic sacrifice, but puts it in context with the whole work of the ministry, according to primitive models and scriptural ideas."

How the commission to dispense the Sacraments "no doubt" includes sacrifice (which is something totally different) I fail to see, and Dr. Gore does not explain. We know the Sacraments of the Prayer Book, and the commission so far is clear. But to sacrifice there is absolutely no reference in the Prayer Book, except when it is rejected in vigorous terms. Dr. Gore needs not to be reminded that the reformers, whether Lutheran, Calvinist, or Zwinglian, denied the Eucharistic sacrifice, while they accepted some Sacraments. The Prayer Book is composed on this principle. Nothing could be more ruthlessly thorough than the excision of the sacrificial expressions which were so numerous in the Catholic books out of which it was to a great extent framed. I am not arguing that the Eucharistic sacrifice cannot now be taught in the Church of England. That is not my affair. I am only too delighted that it should be taught. I do not think that the original sense of the Articles is binding on Bishop Gore, and apart from the Articles there is no positive prohibition of the doctrine. But the *wilful* and complete omission of it has a very serious effect upon the Anglican ordinal.

"Of such a return to antiquity we have no reason to be ashamed, and the Edwardine ordinal makes it abundantly manifest that the office which is being conferred is nothing else than the office of the priesthood. The Pope must, indeed, have been dreaming when he said that 'in the whole ordinal there is no clear mention of . . . the priesthood.'"

The word "priesthood" is here ambiguous. The Pope did not use the word *presbyteratus*, but *sacerdotium*, meaning sacrificial priesthood. He said : "Quamobrem toto ordinali non modo nulla est aperta mentio sacrificii, consecrationis, sacerdotii, potestatisque consecrandi et sacrificii offerendi; sed immo omnia hujusmodi rerum vestigia, quæ superessent in precationibus ritus catholici non plane rejectis, sublata et deleta sunt de industria, quod paulo supra attigimus." The words need no comment, and they are undeniably accurate. Dr. Gore must have been dreaming.

Of the rest of Dr. Gore's remarks I need say nothing. I will go on, however, to some more general considerations which seem to me to be of primary importance.

1. The Catholic Church does not deny the validity of Anglican orders *formaliter et reduplicative*, as the schoolmen have it, in other words, as *Anglican* orders. But she denies that they are *Catholic* orders. The two Archbishops who replied to Leo XIII. merely claimed to have Anglican orders. They put forward a doctrine of the Eucharistic sacrifice which Catholics hold to be heretical. For this sacrifice they declare their orders to be amply sufficient, nor is anyone able to contradict them. But as they did not believe in the Catholic doctrine of sacrifice, they could not assert that their orders enabled them to offer what the Catholic Church means by the word Mass.

The advanced section of the English Church, on the other hand, holds the Catholic view of sacrifice, and claims to have a Catholic priesthood. These persons have, therefore, to reply to the Pope's arguments, which is not strictly necessary for those who take the view of the two Archbishops. To any reader who may have difficulties with regard to any of those arguments, I recommend the *Vindication of the Bull*, published by the Cardinal Archbishop and bishops of the province of Westminster, in which the whole subject is made so clear that it is quite unnecessary for me to touch it.

Dr. Gore seems to hold an intermediate position. He claims that the English Church has true Catholic orders, and he does not reject the Catholic doctrine of the Eucharistic sacrifice. Yet, on the other hand, he is difficult to argue with, because he does not seem wholly to admit Catholic principles. It is not clear that he agrees absolutely even on the subject of sacrifice; he is rather confused about intention, and looks upon the "primitive" view of the priesthood as being "richer and fuller" than what he understands to be the modern Catholic view. This is all so vague that I cannot tell whether the priesthood which he claims, and the principles on which he judges of its validity, are sufficiently near to those which we hold to provide a common ground of argument or not. If his chapter on the subject had been based on the Bull "Apostolicæ curæ" and on the "Vindication" of the Bull, he would no doubt have made his position clearer.

2. There is, however, a general argument against Anglican orders which must not be passed over. The arguments in their favour are satisfactory *to those who are deeply interested in their defence, and to no one else.* The Low Church party to a great extent side with Catholics on the question. The Pope has had the matter carefully considered and all the Anglican pleas fairly weighed, and has been unable to accept them. Provost Maltzew, of Berlin, one of the few Russian theologians whose works are read and appreciated by Western scholars, says that the Orthodox Oriental Church cannot possibly accept Anglican orders as valid. The

Jansenists, of Holland, decided against their validity before the Pope took up the examination of the question.

Thus the Anglican High Church party are left alone in vindicating to themselves powers which they feel to be vital to the position they have taken up. No one is an impartial judge in his own cause, so runs the cynical proverb. There is enough truth in it to make me appeal to Anglican readers to consider whether, after all, their case is as safe as they are in the habit of declaring it to be.

3. It is a principle among Catholic theologians that a probable opinion cannot be followed against the safer view, in those cases where a result has to be certainly attained. In the case of orders which have only probable arguments in favour of their validity they cannot be exercised licitly, because uncertain sacrifices and sacraments are not permissible. Moral certainty, or that certainty which we consider sufficient in grave matters of ordinary life, is needed for the validity of orders if they are to be exercised without sin. Now, however much I may be personally convinced by some theological argument, I cannot call it objectively "morally certain," so long as good authorities hold another view. My own opinion may be morally certain to me, but not necessarily to others. In a question which concerned myself alone I might legitimately act upon it. But where others are concerned, and especially in public actions, I must clearly take the safer course,

and put aside my private opinion. Now, in the case of advanced Anglicans, those above all who deny that the Church of England is more than a somewhat disordered and possibly schismatic province of the Church universal, the validity of their orders is only a private opinion, however firmly established they may personally think it. There is, however, a considerable body of expert opinion on the other side. Condemnations have been repeated many times, and from various quarters. There has apparently been fair inquiry, and there was at least no reason for prejudice. So long as the case stands thus, it does not seem that they ought to exercise their orders.

The case is otherwise with those who, like Bishop Gore, believe more fully in the place and the mission of the Church of England. For them the validity of her orders can be deduced from the fact of her certain position as a national Church. If a Church is clearly neither heretical nor schismatical, there is *primâ facie* ground for expecting, on general grounds of God's good providence, that her orders will be valid. Again, for those who do not accept the Catholic doctrine of sacrifice and of priesthood, there is no cause to submit to judgements delivered on these presuppositions. But for those advanced Anglicans who call themselves the Catholic party, and with whom I have necessarily much sympathy, the case is a grave one whether they ought to exercise their orders in the teeth of so many warnings.

CHAPTER X

ANGLICAN ORTHODOXY

I HAVE very little indeed to say about this chapter. The saying is attributed to Bishop Samuel Wilberforce that orthodoxy is your own doxy, and heterodoxy is the other man's doxy. Dr. Gore's doxy is not mine, and whether he does or does not approve of the teaching of the Anglican Church is of no particular importance except, of course, to himself.

As to giving any opinion myself about Anglican orthodoxy, I should not think of doing such a thing, as I have no idea what doctrines the Church of England officially teaches or denies. The Articles are said not to be definitions. The Prayer Book, if sometimes heretical, is not always consistent. These formularies are interpreted in various ways. One finds Anglicans who maintain that they are allowed to deny Baptismal regeneration, or who complain that they ought not to be forced to accept the Apostles' Creed, or who say the Rosary and have Benediction, and declare that the Vatican Council has œcumenical force. Some are proud of their Church's comprehensiveness, others put it down to an unfortunate relaxation of discipline. It is not for me to say that any of these is wrong, nor is there any tribunal — Convocation, Parliament, the Lambeth Conference — to which I can refer the difficulty.

I am afraid even to say that the Divisibility of the Church is a doctrine of Anglicanism. It is the most fundamental heresy that can

well be conceived, for it does away with the Church and the Rule of Faith. But it has not been defined by any authoritative voice of Anglicanism, nor is it impossible to find Anglicans who admit that they are in schism, though they do not feel themselves bound to emerge from it, so long as they have the hope of delivering their Church as a corporate body from her sinful position.

Dr. Gore has, of course, no mission to speak for the Church of England as a whole. He speaks for a party, or for a part of a party. He has frequently, too frequently, been denounced by High and Low alike, either as a sacerdotalist and a Jesuit in disguise, or as a Nestorian, or as a rationalist. In replying to his book I have avoided any attack upon Anglicanism as a system, because I do not regard it as a system, or upon Anglican doctrine, for it does not appear to have very much compulsory doctrine, or at least I cannot assume that it has, without being at once contradicted on many sides. I have therefore simply replied to Dr. Gore's views, and have defended the Catholic Church, ancient and modern, from his attacks, as best I have been able.

In this chapter he says very little to which I need reply. He thinks that the Church of England teaches a doctrine of the sacraments which he describes on pages 174, 175. Whether he is right or not in attributing just this much to the Church of

England, I do not inquire.[1] From the point of view of Catholic definitions, I must, as he knows, declare, in the first place, his view of the Holy Eucharist to be insufficient, for he says not a word about the substantial change of the bread and wine into the Body and Blood of Christ, although the Fathers so often insist upon this point. He has spoken of the same subject on page 21, where he has quoted, with approval, a beautiful passage from Cardinal Newman on the supra-local nature of our Lord's Presence in the Blessed Sacrament. The doctrine is not the Cardinal's, but St. Thomas of Aquin's.[2] Dr. Gore remarks that "it agrees very ill with some modern practices, attractive as they are, connected with the Tabernacle and the Monstrance." It must be allowed to be *primâ facie* unlikely that the official doctrine of the Church, always so systematic and "logical," should disagree with her practice. I should be glad to supply an explanation of Dr. Gore's difficulty, if he were less vague in his manner of stating it.

As to the correctness of the Anglican doctrine of the sacraments, supposing that he is right in his con-

tention that the acceptance of "two only" is a matter of name (p. 179, note), at least the Church of England has disused two. I will not claim that she brands them as "a corrupt following of the Apostles," but at least she ignores them. She has no Unction of the Sick—which Dr. Gore regrets—even in name ; and she has Confirmation only in name, since she has disused both the matter and the form of the sacrament as they have always been employed in East and West. I do not say this is heresy, for I cannot show that the Church of England rejects these rites—though merely to omit them is bad enough. "These are grave defects—who shall deny it ?" (p. 179).

On page 176 he speaks of the Eucharistic sacrifice. He declares that a doctrine prevailed in the Middle Ages that while the Sacrifice of the Cross was the satisfaction for original sin, the Sacrifice of the Mass is the satisfaction for actual sin. But this is perfectly true doctrine, if properly understood. It *assumes* what no Catholic writer could ever have denied, without being denounced as a heretic, viz. *that all the efficacy of the Sacrifice of the Mass is derived from the Sacrifice of the Cross.* Consequently it asserts that the Sacrifice of the Cross directly and immediately made satisfaction for original sin, while for actual sin satisfaction is made by the daily sacrifice, whose efficacy is from the one absolute Sacrifice. The doctrine does not say that the Sacrifice of the Cross made satisfaction *only* for original sin; it *simply means to exclude original sin from the satisfaction made by the Sacrifice of the Mass.* The passage quoted by Dr. Gore from Pseudo-Albert the Great is therefore perfectly correct, and so is that from the Confession of Augsburg. Dr. Gore is aware

---

[1] I must point out that on page 173 Bishop Gore says : "We can accept the statement of our case from Cardinal Newman," and proceeds to quote a passage in which the Cardinal is stating the case of the Anglicans *before proceeding to refute it.* This might escape the notice of the unwary, for Bishop Gore has so phrased his introduction of Newman's words that it might well be supposed that they stated the Cardinal's own opinion. The reference is to the Preface contributed by him to Hutton's *Anglican Ministry,* page 8, a Preface which Dr. Gore has on page 148, note, called "surely very unworthy of its great author"—apparently because it contains some very unpleasant home truths.

[2] *Summa Th.*, iii., qu. 76, art. 5, 6. The most elaborate explanation of it that I know of is in Suarez, *Disp.* 53 *in* 3 *Part. S. Thomæ.*

that the Lutherans who drew up that Confession rejected the Sacrifice of the Altar altogether, and this passage is denying the Catholic doctrine of the time. But it is misleading in expression, for there are other ways of applying the satisfaction made once by Christ—penance, internal and external—good works—indulgences. The quotation from Latimer is just the coarse caricature of Catholic doctrine that we expect from such a man. Nevertheless this mediæval way of expressing the truth was incautious, and liable to misrepresentation. I do not know that it has been employed since the Council of Trent. [1]

[1] On the other hand, Dr. Gore's own doctrine of Sacrifice is imperfectly expressed. He says (p. 177): "The Eucharist is not even mystically a *renewal* of Christ's passion, but an act of co-operation with Christ's heavenly intercession. Christ upon the Eucharistic altar is only 'offered' in the sense that His once made sacrifice is there perpetually presented and pleaded before the Father, as in heaven, so on earth. The altar is, so to speak, on a line not with Calvary, but with the heavenly Intercession." The second of these three sentences may pass. The first and third are false. As in heaven it is the Body once slain, marked with its wounds, which is ever presented, so upon earth the *two-fold consecration* is the "representation" as well as the "re-presentation" of the Sacrifice of Calvary. It is therefore not really, but "mystically," a *renewal* of the one all-sufficient Sacrifice. But I have never liked Franzelin's doctrine of the Eucharistic sacrifice, because I have always thought that it necessarily makes each Mass add something to the Sacrifice of the Cross, which would be heresy. Of course, Franzelin would vehemently deny this, but I am not surprised to find Dr. Gore somewhat shocked at the apparent consequences of the doctrine, in his note on page 177. The passage which he adds from a devotional book *is not intended to be taken seriously* or it would be blasphemous. What is the good of high-flown exaggerations of this sort, which cannot be understood literally, I am unable to imagine. But the pious author no doubt meant extremely little by what he considered to be eloquence.

On page 79 begins a long paragraph in which Bishop Gore declares that the Church of England has indeed lost much, but desires the restoration of all she has lost. I am afraid Bishop Gore is too sanguine —I wish to God he may be right.

But on page 181 Dr. Gore turns round upon the "Church of Rome," and there is nothing in the Church of England more regrettable to him than certain things he finds in it:

1. The withdrawal of the chalice from all but the officiating priest. If this were really a ground of complaint, surely *some* Catholic theologians would be found inclined to urge a change of the long-established Catholic usage of communion in one kind, surely *some* of the laity would beg for a restoration of the supposed privilege. But nothing of the sort. We are all agreed within the Catholic Church that doctrinally the practice is correct, that the communicant suffers no loss, and that as a matter both of reverence and of convenience the practice is supremely proper and almost inevitable. If communion in both kinds was a Divine command, or if communion in one kind was a lesser grace, then of course the question of reverence would be irrelevant. But as it is, I am glad not to witness now the unavoidable spilling of the sacred element down the sides of the chalice and over the fingers of the officiant, which is unavoidable in the Anglican system. I confess that before I became a Catholic I longed for the introduction of communion in one kind into the Anglican Church. The Eastern method would partly avoid this difficulty, but it would remain almost impossible in practice to communicate the multitudes of the Catholic Church in this manner. When a priest cannot calculate within a hundred or so (this is very common,

even in England) how many communicants there will be, how can he tell how much wine to consecrate? He cannot reserve what remains unconsumed, though he could add wine if the quantity was insufficient.[1]

Communion out of Mass would be impossible in both kinds, and yet in many cases there is no other way of giving the Sacrament to a large number of the people. These difficulties do not arise among Anglicans, because communions are so rare. The *Year Book of the Church of England* estimates all the communicants in England at less than two millions. Of a Catholic town in Germany, in which the number of people of an age to go to Holy Communion is about 30,000, I am told on good authority that (excluding religious communities, since their communions are frequent in the week) the number of communions in the year is 250,000. The number at the one church of Einsiedeln is 170,000 in the year. These are the only statistics I happen to know; I give them merely to show how practically impossible it would be to combine the modern practice of frequent communion with communion in both kinds.

2. "I have never heard a sermon in an English church more to be regretted than one it was once my lot to hear in Strasburg Cathedral, in which Christ was preached as the revelation of Divine Justice and Mary as the revelation of Divine Love." I confess I am a little incredulous about this. I suspect some exaggeration and misunderstanding, though of course preachers *do* say stupid things. But Dr. Gore misunderstands or interprets in a

bad sense even what he finds in print. It is easier to put a harsh construction on what one hears in a foreign language.

3. "I have not read in Anglican biography anything which I should more desire to disown than Mother Margaret Mary Hallahan's description of the Pope singing Mass. 'When I heard him sing Mass I cannot express what I felt; it was the God of earth prostrate in adoration before the God of heaven.'" The book referred to is a very beautiful book indeed. It is not the life of a canonised saint, but I should indeed be glad if such a life could be matched among Anglican biographies! Mother Margaret's motto was "God alone," and she seems to have been full of the thought of Him at all moments. Even on this great occasion in St. Peter's it was not the ceremonies, the pomp, the music, the enthusiastic multitudes which touched her most, but the thought of the immense honour done to God by the most solemn offering of Mass possible on earth by the highest dignity on earth. Her expression is energetic. I cannot see that it is objectionable from any point of view. I cannot imagine that Bishop Gore can think she meant "the God of earth" as a definition of the Pope's status in the world!

4. Next Dr. Gore quotes an extremely silly parody of the *Anima Christi*, applied to our Blessed Lady. I should not wish to employ it. But I have no wish to disown it, as it contains no false doctrine. The invocations are simply poetical licences (in both senses of the word). In the original *Anima Christi* we do not invoke, though we adore, the Soul, Body, and Passion of Christ. Similarly "Soul of the Virgin, save me; Body of the Virgin, guard me; Milk of the

[1] I need hardly say that we regard the Anglican method of repeating *one* of the consecrations without the other as a grave sacrilege.

Virgin, feed me," either means nothing at all, or it means, "Thy Soul is immaculate and full of grace, thy Body was preserved from corruption, thy Milk fed the Son of God

—pray for me, who recall these privileges." There is no harm in this ; but Dr. Gore should have quoted it in Latin, for the English version he has made is indecent.

CHAPTER XI

THREE RECENT PAPAL UTTERANCES

1. *THE Encyclical (of 1893) on "The Study of Sacred Scripture."*

Bishop Gore thinks that the late Pope in this Encyclical of twelve years ago took too narrow a view of Inspiration. Catholic theologians will not agree with the implication (p. 188) that Leo XIII. has denied the word *auctor* in the decrees of the Vatican, of Trent, and of a whole series of previous councils to mean "primary cause" (of course not "primary cause" in the sense that God is the primary cause of everything, but in a special sense). In the Vatican decree the meaning "literary author" might conceivably be understood, were it not that this meaning is impossible in the earlier decrees which this decree repeats.

Again, Bishop Gore finds in the Encyclical an assertion of "verbal inspiration." There are a few Catholic theologians who take this view, but the greater number would certainly not think that this was the Pope's intention. For myself, though I am inclined to agree with the Abbot of Downside[1] that "verbal inspiration" is not merely the oldest view, but the view which leaves the theologian most free to deal with difficulties, yet I feel unable to agree with the Abbot that

Leo XIII. can possibly have intended to condemn other opinions commonly taught by Catholic theologians of to-day. I cannot see that the Pope's words imply verbal inspiration : " By supernatural power, He so moved and impelled them to write—He was so present to them —that the things which He ordered, and those only, they first rightly understood, then willed faithfully to write down, and finally expressed in apt words and with infallible truth." It is difficult to see how any theory of inspiration could say *less* than this.

On the other hand, Dr. Gore is right in pointing out that the Encyclical excludes all possibility of error of every kind in inspired writings. But he must remember that *substantial error* is intended. Nobody supposes that the Evangelists give the discourses of our Lord word for word ! There are many more important discrepancies. I will not go into this matter, as I do not wish to air my own theories. I will simply instance St. Augustine's explanation that the Centurion's coming to our Lord (in St. Matthew) is the same thing as the coming of a messenger from the Centurion (in St. Luke), for what a man does by means of another he may be said to do himself.[2] How far can

[1] In the *Tablet.* January 14th to February 4th, 1905.

[2] *De Consensu Evang.*, 20, read in the Breviary the day after Ash Wednesday.

this principle be extended? How far again, can the principle be extended that the historian in Genesis (for example) does not vouch for the history he relates? How much can we infer from the inconsistency of 1 Maccabees with 2 Maccabees?

Many of the early genealogies in Genesis are genealogies of tribes, not of nations. Nobody supposes the chronology to be historical. How far is this to carry us? It is at least clear that substantial error is not to be found in inspired writers in cases where they, in their own person, relate facts of which they vouch for the truth. It is good that the Pope should have reminded us of this. If it were not so, we should be reduced to mere human authority for the facts of our Lord's life, and our belief in them would be limited by our ability to prove the accuracy of the evangelists. We may make their accuracy highly probable by human investigations, but we cannot make it certain in any particular case. Yet many of the actions and events in the Gospels are as important as the direct teachings, while we do not wish to renounce our faith in any of them. It is unimportant for us to know whether our Lord was going into Jericho or coming out of it when He healed two blind men. It does not matter whether a voice from Heaven said to our Lord: "Thou art My beloved Son," or to St. John Baptist: "This is My beloved Son."[1] But we should not like to be obliged to doubt many beautiful details, where there is no divergence in the accounts. Dr. Gore's idea that the Pope attributes the whole

Pentateuch to Moses (p. 194) is an imagination of his own.

Dr. Gore also refers to the suppression of the periodical *L'enseignement biblique*. It was judged by Rome that the periodical was doing harm. It appears that Rome was more right than Dr. Gore, for M. Loisy, whose articles were the cause of the suppression, has since shown himself in a reply to Dr. Harnack's *What is Christianity?* to be more radical in his views than the rationalist writer whom he is attacking. It is well known that the best Anglican critics have little admiration for M. Loisy's imprudences, and are not surprised at the condemnation of *L'Evangile et l'Eglise*. But let us remember that the condemnation of some books of Loisy's only so far amounts to a statement that they are dangerous, or disedifying, or liable to be misunderstood. What precisely is censured, and in what degree, has not been expressed.

It is true that a few bad Catholics, anonymously or under their own name, have been complaining in Protestant periodicals that Rome is trying to suppress all intellectual freedom in the Church. What I have to complain of in these writers is the extreme ignorance they invariably show (in the cases which have come under my notice) of the subjects on which they write so glibly.[2]

Now I turn to Dr. Gore's expectation expressed in his first chapter, page 22:—

"God has, we must believe, special tasks in store for the Anglican Church,

---

[1] The Western reading in St. Matthew, "This day have I begotten Thee," I have reasons for regarding as a correction to suit Psalm ii., for there are parallels for such an act. The date of the correction is very early indeed.

[2] It should be recollected that any Roman decisions must *necessarily* be on the conservative side, for they simply guard the definitions of the Church. But this does not mean that only conservative views are encouraged by Rome! Reactionaries are often more dangerous than liberals, but they seldom give a handle to enable authority to condemn them.

tasks for which the Roman temper and the Roman theology are by their very character and tone disqualified. To some of these we have alluded. It seems likely that it will belong to us, rather than to Rome, to work out the relations of religion to critical knowledge, and to vindicate the true character of inspiration in its relation to historical research."

I cannot imagine an expectation more impossible of realisation. In the Anglican communion there are all sorts of views as to inspiration, and there is absolutely no authority to direct, assist, approve them. The divergences may possibly increase; it is quite improbable that they will tend to lessen. More and more individuals will propose solutions. They may form into schools, but there is no reasonable expectation of their arriving at any one agreement.

On the other hand, the Catholic Church gives a certain amount of direction and assistance to her children—not very much, it is true, but at least when it is most needed. The stores of the past are being examined and debated by theologians, while the critics are using their scalpels. *All work in common, all are contributing to a common result,* and the materials supplied by those without are all utilised. Gradually the question will grow clearer. Some day, perhaps, if necessity arises, even new definitions may be given. But, in any case, discussion and examination are converging to a result, and not (as amongst Anglicans) resulting in divergence. Dr. Gore considers that a document more out of date, more crude, more unsympathetic, more unpastoral than the Encyclical on Holy Scripture could not have been issued. It needs a special training to understand the bearing of Roman documents and decrees.

Dr. Gore has certainly not understood the Encyclical. I will merely remark upon two important facts:—

(i.) Catholic theologians have become more free in their treatment of Holy Scripture since the decree was issued twelve years ago, although they have habitually started from its teaching.

(ii.) Instead of suppressing the free study of Scripture, the Encyclical appears to have been the cause of the remarkable efflorescence of biblical study in recent years among Catholics, especially within the last two or three years. I daresay this has hardly yet been noticed much in England. In a few years I think it will be patent to the world at large that the Catholic Church is ceasing to take the secondary place in critical study of the Old and New Testaments, which she certainly occupied before the appearance of the Encyclical.

There were many reasons for this undoubted abstention of Catholics from such critical problems. I will mention one. The Tübingen School, and similar manifestations of German ingenuity in the middle of the nineteenth century, were too extreme and too fanciful to be a pressing danger to Catholics. The peril was first brought home to the Continental Catholics by Renan's *Life of Christ,* as it was to the English world by *Supernatural Religion.* There was at the moment no protagonist capable of taking the field with Renan on equal terms, and a generation was needed to bring the question into prominence. Now that German views are more moderate, it is possible (as Dr. Gore pointed out on the day of his enthronisation as bishop of Birmingham) for Catholics to work together with scholars of all schools for the elucidation of critical problems. The need for warding off more insidious dangers is now more urgent, while the new generation is more ready for the work; and at the same time it is possible to avoid controversy and help in a sort of co-operative society towards the attainment of more certain materials for the solution of the difficulties which lie before us. But the Catholic has three immense advantages. He has tradition behind him; he has the Church to warn him off from dangerous paths, and he has the fellowship of those who are working with the same aims and the same principles towards a common agreement.

2. *The Encyclical on Unity,* "*Satis Cognitum*" (1896). I have already said enough about the unity of the Church. I need only deal here with Dr. Gore's accusation of "wholly unhistorical assertions."

The Pope said: "The consent of antiquity ever acknowledged without the slightest doubt or hesitation the bishops of Rome, and revered them as the legitimate successors of St. Peter." Dr. Gore hereupon re-iterates his assertion that "the papal claim of the succession to Petrine privileges is a purely Western growth," and this time he is more confident than he was on page 91. I have already replied to this: the assertion is utterly groundless. Dr. Gore then quotes from Janus (!): "In the writings of the Greek doctors, Eusebius, St. Athanasius, St. Basil the Great, the two Gregories, and St. Epiphanius, there is not one word of any [unique] prerogative of the Roman bishop." Dr. Gore has done his best to correct the characteristic-ally impudent statement of Janus into something more tolerable by the insertion of a word, but he has not succeeded in making it true. Even the references given above, here and there, to Eusebius will show that he is full of references to the unique position of the Roman bishop. I have shown above that St. Athanasius was a sort of "Ultra-montane" of his day. In St. Basil there is certainly not much to quote on the subject; in St. Gregory Nazianzen there is less. The state-ment is absolutely true only with regard to St. Gregory of Nyssa and St. Epiphanius. What does this prove? That they disagreed with St. Athanasius? There is absolutely no reason why they should have said a word upon the subject. There are plenty of modern Catholic writers since the Vatican Council in whose theological writings not a single word on the subject can be found. If Dr. Gore wanted to prove anything, he ought to have been able to say: "Eusebius, St. Athanasius, St. Basil, the two Gregories, all denied that the bishop of Rome possessed any unique prerogative, although the claims made by the popes of the fourth century are well known." But Dr. Gore knows that he cannot say this. But unless he says this or something similar, he cannot re-fute the assertion of Pope Leo XIII.

But though Dr. Gore does not claim to be logical, it is well for us to notice that the sentence quoted from the Encyclical says not a word about any unique prerogative of the popes; it merely says they were acknowledged as the "legitimate successors of St. Peter." He did not choose a good quotation on which to hang his remarks.

"What, again, is the meaning of saying that 'it has ever been un-questionably the office of the Roman pontiffs to ratify or to reject the decrees of councils,' when as late as the fifteenth-century Council of Con-stance the subordination of popes to councils was unmistakably asserted as the doctrine of the Church?"

What an ignorant man Pope Leo must have been, not to know that the Councils of Basle and Constance asserted that the councils were above the Pope!

Really, this is rather amusing. Does not Bishop Gore know that in the thirteenth century this view would have been called heresy? Is he really unaware that it arose during the troubles of the Great Schism of the West? It was inevitable, when a council was the only means of deciding who was Pope, that the papal prerogatives should suffer, and that the council should exalt itself above the popes whom it seemed to judge. The councils of the fifteenth century have only been confirmed by papal authority in part. Part of their decisions, including this particular point, were undoubtedly heretical. A moderate form of the same view was taken up by the Gallicans, but was never tolerated at Rome. So much for Dr. Gore's proof from the supposed survival up to the sixteenth century of a doctrine of the superiority of a council to the Pope.

But what of antiquity?

To begin with, the Council of Constantinople, in 381, is œcumenical, because it was approved by the Pope; it was originally only a council of the East. On the other hand, in 359, an œcumenical council was assembled for convenience as two councils, the one at Seleucia, the other at Ariminum. The decrees published were heretical. Both were condemned by Pope Liberius,[1] and Catholicity was saved.

In 450, an œcumenical council was held at Ephesus. It decreed Monophysitism. Pope Leo condemned it, and again the truth was saved. I have shown in chapter vii. that the supremacy of

the Pope was admitted both at the œcumenical council of Ephesus, in 431, and that of Chalcedon, in 451.[2] I have also shown (ch. iii.) that the Greek historians of the fifth century declare it to have been an ecclesiastical rule in the fourth century that the Churches could not make canons without the consent of the bishop of Rome (I need hardly say that this does not refer to local decisions). We have seen that the bishops of Africa, in 417, regarded the Pope's decisions in a matter of faith as more binding and more likely to be obeyed than those of two African councils of more than 120 bishops, and St. Augustine declares the Pope's reply to the councils to be final, and St. Prosper (or a contemporary) allows binding force to the decrees of the councils, because the popes had "made them their own by approving them."

Flavian, bishop of Constantinople, when condemned by the Robber-Council of Ephesus (which was intended to be œcumenical), in 450, appealed from the decision, and the legate Hilarus (afterward Pope) rose and uttered the word: "Κοντρα-δίκιτουρ" (Mansi, vi. 507). When this was read at Chalcedon, the Fathers cried: "Anathema to Dioscorus! Long live Leo!" In the next year Theodoret appealed to St. Leo for the removal of the

[1] So St. Siricius, P.L., xiii. p. 1133.

[2] St. Cyril says in his letter to Acacius of Melitene (Mansi, v. 326) of Sixtus III., the successor of Celestine: If Acacius is told that a letter was brought from Sixtus disapproving of the deposition of Nestorius, he must not believe it. "For he wrote what was in accord with the holy synod, and *confirmed all its acts*, and is in agreement with us." Celestine had died in July, 432. The testimony of the sixth and seventh general councils is still more decisive for the papal authority. Each simply accepted the letter of a Pope as a final decision.

suspension under which he had been for twenty years; it had been inflicted by no less an authority than the Council of Ephesus. The Pope absolved him. At Chalcedon the sincerity of the bishop was tested by insisting on his anathematising Nestorius. When he consented, his restoration was agreed to with acclamations and cries of "Long live Leo! Leo has judged with God" (Mansi, vii. 189).

Nothing is so important in this question to a Catholic as the assurance that the popes themselves have always taught that they are above councils. I will quote four :—

St. Damasus, to the bishops of Illyricum and the East: "No prejudice can arise on account of the number of those who assembled at Ariminum, since it is known that *neither the Roman bishop, whose opinion was to be inquired before all,* nor Vincentius, nor others of the same merit, gave any assent to the decisions."

St. Zosimus, 417: "Although the tradition of the Fathers has attributed to the Apostolic see so great authority that none would dare to contest its judgements," etc. (*Ep.* 12).

St. Boniface I., in 422 : "For it has *never been allowed* to discuss again what has once been decided by the Apostolic see" (*Ep.* 13).

St. Leo, of the 28th Council of Chalcedon : "We make it void, and by the authority of St. Peter the Apostle, by a wholly general definition we annul it" (*Ep.* 105).

I do not think it necessary to quote later popes, as I imagine that nobody doubts their opinion.

But as Dr. Gore thinks the Western Church held an opposite view until the fifteenth century, I will quote two later writers :—

Ferrandus of Carthage, *c.* 530: "The Apostolic see, *by the consent of which, whatever that synod* (Chalcedon) *defined, has received invincible strength*" (*P. L.*, 67, 925).

St. Avitus, bishop of Vienne, to two Roman Senators, when Pope Symmachus was accused before a Roman council: "It is not easy to understand on what ground or by what law a superior is judged by his inferiors. . . Love not less in your Church the Chair of Peter, than in your city the metropolis of the world" (*Ep.* 31).

I do not know that there is any room for hesitation as to the truth of Pope Leo's words.

Now I come to Leo XIII.'s "unjustifiable quotations."

"The Pope quotes St. Pacian as saying, 'To Peter the Lord spake ; to one therefore, that he might establish unity upon one.' But he omits to mention that he continues, 'and soon he was to give the same injunction to the general body'" (p. 199).

In fact the Pope omits all the rest of St. Pacian's writings ! Why should he not? St. Pacian is here using the celebrated passage of St. Cyprian on which I have commented above (ch. v.). The words added by Dr. Gore are the anticipation of a possible objection, as are in St. Cyprian the similar expressions, and they were wholly irrelevant to the Pope's purpose. Does Dr. Gore really think St. Pacian meant us to supply mentally "in order that he might establish multiplicity upon many?"

"He cites, in confirmation of the papal view of Peter as the rock, some quite ambiguous words of Origen, although the passage cited above (p. 86) immediately precedes."

I have shown above (p. 57) that it is Dr. Gore who has unaccountably (or through prejudice) misrepresented Origen's meaning.

"He cites Cyprian as saying, 'of the Roman Church that it is the root and mother of the Catholic Church, the Chair of Peter, and the principal Church, whence sacerdotal unity had its origin.' This is a combination of two different passages, of which the first, 'the root and mother of the Catholic Church,' has no reference to the Roman Church, and the second, from a letter strongly rebuking the Pope, refers to Rome as the source of the Apostolical Succession in Africa" (p. 199).

I am inclined to agree with Dr. Gore that "the root and mother" in *Ep.* 48, 3, does not mean the Roman Church. But the Pope was surely justified in taking it in this sense, as many of the best Protestant critics have done, for instance, Neander, Sohm, Harnack! The second quotation is not "from a letter rebuking the Pope," it is from a letter to Pope Cornelius (*Ep.* 59, 4) to thank him for having excommunicated Felicissimus, to encourage him not to be terrified by the threats of his (Cyprian's) adversaries, for he thought Cornelius had shown signs of weakness. He goes on to defend his own right to the episcopate in an eloquent passage, and the rest of the letter is chiefly concerned with a refutation of the claims of the rival bishop of Carthage, Fortunatus. The idea that *unde unitas sacerdotalis exorta est* can mean that Rome is the source of the "Apostolical Succession" in Africa shows that Dr. Gore has not studied St. Cyprian's doctrine of the origin of the episcopate from St Peter.

"Now I may fairly ask whether the accusations of inveracity and disingenuousness which have been made in the course of this book against the Roman method of argument are not again justified."

If Dr. Gore had proved that the Pope was wrong, he might have concluded that he was ignorant, but not that he was disingenuous—that would be a quite uncertain inference. I do not make it in Dr. Gore's case. I am sorry the former inference is not always to be avoided.

3. *The Bull "Apostolicæ Curæ."*

I have sufficiently dealt with this, under the head of "Anglican Ordinations," in chapter ix.

PAPAL INFALLIBILITY

I add here some explanations which Dr. Gore needs. On pages 192, 193 he is uncertain whether papal infallibility extends to Encyclicals or not. The answer is of course in the negative, as a general rule. It is not supposed that a Pope speaks *ex cathedra* except in a solemn definition, usually under anathema. For instance, the Bull in which Pope Pius IX. defined the Immaculate Conception, *Ineffabilis Deus*, is infallible, not throughout, but only in the formal conclusion at which it arrives: " *Auctoritate Domini Nostri Jesu Christi, beatorum Apostolorum Petri et Pauli ac Nostra declaramus, pronunciamus et definimus.*" The same view is applied to councils as well as popes. The *Capitula* of the Council of Trent are to be regarded as commentaries of the highest authority on the canons, but they are not strictly exercises of the Church's infallibility, for they are not definitions. The *canons* are infallible, for they are imposed under anathema. Similarly an Encyclical is a kind of sermon, not a definition.

I have said above that I do not wish to interpret the strong expressions found in the fourth and fifth centuries as equivalent to the dogma of Papal Infallibility as at present understood. They cover it indeed, but they are too wide. The *Tractatoria* of Pope Zosimus was a very lengthy document, and was regarded as a final decision on the Pelagian question. To-day such a document would have its pith summed up in a few carefully worded phrases. The "tome" of St. Leo is another instance of the diffuseness with which ancient Popes defined the faith. The infallibility of Rome, the infallibility of papal censures on matters of faith, receive very early testimony, but only gradually were papal "definitions" involved. St. Leo apparently meant his "tome" to Flavian as an infallible utterance, but in the case of a document of that length I do not see that he could have complained if the Fathers of Chalcedon had objected to the wording here and there as ambiguous or misleading. As a fact, St. Leo thought it was the devil who made some bishops ask for explanations![1]

[1] "Our help is in the name of the Lord, who made heaven and earth, who has not permitted us to suffer any loss in our brethren, but *what He had first defined by our ministry*, He has confirmed by the irretractable assent of the whole of our brotherhood, so as to show that what was first formulated by the first of all sees, and was then accepted by the judgement of the whole Christian world, truly proceeded from Him; that in this also the members might concord with the head. And in this we have the greater matter for rejoicing, since the enemy has wounded himself the more, in that he the more savagely arose against the Ministers of Christ. For lest the agreement of the other sees with that one which the Lord of all appointed to preside over the rest might seem mere acquiescence, or lest any other adverse suspicion should arise, *there were first found some to doubt about our judgements*. And when some were incited by the author of dissensions to commence a war of contradiction, by the dispensation of the author of all good we arrived at a greater good" (St. Leo, *Ep.* 120, to Theodoret).

On page 124 Dr. Gore finds some "'difficulties' in the way of believing in the infallibility of the bishop of Rome," besides the cases of Liberius and Honorius already mentioned. He gives three which he considers to be "of overwhelming magnitude."

"Nicholas I. assured the Bulgarians that Baptism in the name of Christ only was valid." But this is not a definition of Faith.[2]

"Eugenius IV., in his instruction to the Armenians, makes the 'porrection of the instruments' the essential matter of order." Again this is not a definition of Faith.

"Nicholas II. compelled Berengarius to acknowledge the Capernaite heresy that Christ's body is *sensibly* (sensualiter) touched by the hands and broken by the teeth in the Eucharist." He did nothing of the kind, nor is this imaginary "Capernaite heresy" known to history—no one has ever actually held that our Lord's Body is present in the Blessed Sacrament *in a natural manner.* The words submitted to Berengarius are "panem et vinum post consecrationem non solum sacramentum, sed etiam verum corpus et verum sanguinem Domini nostri Jesu Christi esse, et sensualiter *non solum in sacramento sed et in veritate manibus sacerdotum tractari, frangi et fidelium dentibus atteri.*" Obviously this is naturally patient of an absurd interpretation. But the real translation of the last words is as follows: "The true Body and Blood . . . are not in a figure only, but in truth that which is sensibly touched by the hands of the priests, broken and crushed by the teeth of

[2] Nicholas is quoting St. Ambrose. Both writers *probably* mean that baptism "in the name of Christ," as mentioned in Acts, is *the same as* baptism in the name of the Holy Trinity, *i.e.* that it implies the use of the Trinitarian formula. But this is not quite certain.

the faithful." The true meaning is amply proved by the controversies of the time to be that *there is no other substance* which is the subject of these actions; but it was not supposed that anyone could import the idea that the Body of Christ is naturally broken in two in heaven when the accidents of bread are broken, or that the whole Body is not present in each part after fraction. Hence the carelessness of the wording. It was important to avoid the subterfuges by which Berengarius tried to escape condemnation without admitting the doctrine of the Church. The Body of Christ is touched when the accidents of bread are touched, but *per accidens*, not directly. It was not anticipated that anyone would be so perverse as to suppose that it could be thought that the Body of Christ is immediately touched any more than it is immediately seen! If it was immediately touched, its texture would be felt by the hand that touched it, just as its appearance would be perceived, if it was immediately seen. Yet it is both common and correct to speak of touching, tasting, breaking the Body of Christ. So speaks, for example, the great doctor of the Holy Eucharist, St. John Chrysostom : "For Christ has given to us nothing sensible, but in sensible things what is spiritually discerned," and then almost immediately : "How many now say—Would that I could see His form, His likeness, His garments, His shoes ! Behold, *thou seest Him, thou touchest Him, thou eatest Him*" (*Hom.* 82, 4, *in Matt.*). Or again : "Why did he add, 'Which we break ?' For this we can see happen at the Eucharist ; but not upon the cross, but rather the contrary ; for 'a bone of Him,' it was said, 'shall not be broken.' *But what He did not suffer upon the cross, this He suffers in the Oblation for thy sake, and bears to be broken in half* (ἀνέχεται διακλώμενος) that He may fill all" (*Hom.* 24, 2, *in* 1 *Cor.*). I do not think these passages need apology or explanation.

"These difficulties," Dr. Gore concludes, "are only examples." It follows, then, that the rest are not very serious, and he did well not to bring them forward.

CHAPTER XII

EPILOGUE

I.

WE have hitherto followed Dr. Gore chapter by chapter. Let us look at the antitheses at which we have arrived.

1. I am a Catholic because I belong to the Catholic Church—the Church diffused throughout the world. Bishop Gore refuses to believe that there exists *a Church throughout the world.* The Church in which he believes is a Church of the future, an ideal *in fieri*, for it consists of the departed in "Paradise," of those who are not yet born, as well as of a great many people still alive—but this latter class does not constitute "a separate unity,"[1] *i.e.* a Church throughout the world.

On the other hand, he does be-

[1] See his note, p. 33.

lieve in " Churches " throughout the world, though he apparently does not include among these the Protestant communities of Scandinavia, Germany, Switzerland, America, etc., nor the English and Welsh Nonconformists.

2. The Catholic Church teaches that she must be and always is one—and " visibly " one in the same sense in which she is a "visible" body. This is practically the same as the first point—there is a body throughout the world which is, and has always been, the one Catholic Church. Bishop Gore thinks it has split into fragments.

3. The Church is not only Catholic and one, she is Apostolic—she retains the right to teach which was given to the Apostles, and she retains their authority—she is infallible in teaching, and absolute in authority. According to Dr. Gore, these attributes ceased after a few centuries, and the Church has no longer a voice which can compel assent or obedience.

4. It is very wonderful to see in history this One Catholic and Apostolic Church majestically proceeding through the centuries. It is more wonderful to contemplate her sanctity—that of her teaching, and that of her children. Of this, Dr. Gore prudently says nothing. I do not wish to deny or to minimise the claims of the Russian Church to have produced saints in her schism. A schism caused by political motives, and involving practically no heresy, may well be expected to bear much good fruit. Let us make the most of the many estimable men whom Anglicanism, and Lutheranism, and Wesleyanism, etc., have produced—it would be, indeed, shocking if such were not found wherever the doctrines of the New Testament are studied with reverence.

But the multitude of the saints—the miraculous saints, the heroes of penance and charity, of missionary enterprise and cloistered meditation, bishops and laymen, martyrs and confessors, monks and virgins—these belong to the one Catholic and Apostolic Church. To her God gives His choicest gifts; on her alone He lavishes the marvels of grace which He deals out more sparingly to others.

But I go further. The ordinary means of attaining holiness are infinitely greater in her than in any other body. It is not only that her sacraments are surely valid. She has the tradition, the methods, the true doctrine. The tradition and the methods,—for she is full of the institutions of the saints—her laws, her customs, her monasteries and houses of charity, her ways, her peculiarities, her systems, are theirs. In her alone are the innumerable daily Masses, the frequent Communions, the multiplied and various forms of holy devotions for all classes and all characters. If Dr. Gore wants spiritual reading for himself or others, he will take in hand some manual " adapted " from a Catholic source. If he wishes to learn methods of direction of souls, to know the experience of ages, he will betake himself to a Catholic ascetical writer, and so forth.

But also the true doctrine. Dr. Gore has made the interesting assertion (p. 11): "A man cannot be at home in the current Roman doctrine of ' good works ' and in St. Paul's Epistles." I have not the least idea—I say it truthfully—what Dr. Gore supposes "the current Roman doctrine of good works" to be. I do know that the immoral antinomianism of Luther has left its spell over every part of Protestantism. Thank God, there are revivalists and salvationists who teach men to repent and begin new lives. Would that they could do more for their perseverance. Thank God, there are many clergymen of the Anglican body who urge men to confession, contrition, and amendment. But alas that "church going" and "thoughtful sermons" on subjects of the day should be the main part of the spiritual food offered to our countrymen! What does the average Englishman know of sin, of sorrow, of amendment, of falls, of resolutions, of perseverance? He does not know his need, he does not heed his destitution of help, and he is, therefore, fortunately less accountable than a bad Catholic would be.

But if Dr. Gore were inside the Catholic communion, he would find there a practical "doctrine of good works" well known to all the faithful. They believe that they will be judged at the last day by their works, and that they must anticipate the judgement here, if they are to escape in that day. If a man wishes to be a practising Catholic, he knows that he must give up sin. If he does not wish to give up sin, he does not go to confession. Who does not know the root of much of the supposed rationalism in Catholic countries? When a man who has persecuted the Church by his vote and his influence, on his death-bed sends for the priest—as so often happens, thank God—he acknowledges thereby that it has not been a rooted conviction, but some worldly motive, that has kept him from the practice of his religious duties; and in how many cases the simple explanation is that he has not had the courage to change his life?

The Catholic Church teaches that God intends us to be like Himself, and she tries to make us like Him, and nobody can be a practising Catholic without in some measure trying to be like Him.

If there were nothing else known to me of the Catholic Church but her system of confession, as I know it by experience, it would be enough alone to prove to me her divine origin.

But words are of little use. I cannot make others see what I see. Those outside do not *see* the Church; they see men, they see doctrines, they see facts of history—but they cannot see the wood for the trees. Yet the Church is God's witness that He it is who sent Jesus Christ: "that the world may believe that Thou hast sent Me." This witness is not revealed to all. In Catholic countries it is clear enough, and everyone is either a Catholic or an opponent of Christianity. But in a land like England it is hard for those who have been born and reared and educated in heresy and in prejudice to get to the vision of the one Catholic Church. Tichonius, the Donatist, says St. Augustine, "aroused by all the voices of the holy pages, awoke and beheld the Church of God diffused throughout the whole world, even as it had been foreseen and foretold of her so long before by the hearts and the mouths of the saints."[1] That is the point: *Evigilavit et vidit*, "He awoke and beheld." As with the ancient African scholar, so with a modern student of the Fathers, to whom Robert Wilberforce pointed out a short sentence from the very treatise of St. Augustine which I have quoted: "He repeated the words again and again, and when he was gone they kept ringing in my ear. '*Securus judicat orbis terrarum.*' . . ." "The entire world judges *with security* that they are not good who separate themselves from the entire world, in whatever part of the entire world."[2] The

[1] *C. litt Parm.* i. 1.
[2] *C. litt. Parm.* iii. 3.

words are simple enough, though I do not think Dr. Gore has seen what they mean. But their meaning came as a flash upon Newman after his long studies and anxieties.

"They were words which went beyond the occasion of the Donatists: they applied to that of the Monophysites. They decided ecclesiastical questions on a simpler rule than that of antiquity; nay, St. Augustine was one of the prime oracles of antiquity; here then antiquity was deciding against itself.
"Who can account for the impressions which are made on him? For a mere sentence, the words of St. Augustine struck me with a power which I had never felt from any words before. To take a familiar instance, they were like the 'Turn again, Whittington' of the chime; or, to take a more serious one, they were like the 'Tolle, lege—Tolle, lege,' of the child, which converted St. Augustine himself. '*Securus judicat orbis terrarum.*' By those great words of the ancient Father, interpreting and summing up the long and varied course of ecclesiastical history, the theory of the *Via Media* was absolutely pulverized."[1]

Why this extraordinary state of mind? "Dismay and disgust"— "dreadful misgivings"—"It has given me a stomach-ache!"[2] "I had seen the shadow of a hand upon the wall." "He who has seen a ghost cannot be as if he had never seen it. The heavens had opened and closed again."
Evigilavit et vidit. He had awakened and had beheld that Church for which the Son of God had prayed: "That they may be one, that the world may know that Thou hast sent Me."[3]

[1] Newman, *Apologia*, ch. 3.
[2] Newman, *Letters and Correspondence*, vol. ii. p. 286.
[3] John xvii. 21. Cp. John xi. 42: "And I know that Thou hearest Me always."

II.

Thus we differ about the Church. So again Dr. Gore takes a view of the history of Christianity which differs by the whole of heaven from the Catholic view.

He sees a providence in that history, but all is natural. God set a truth in the world, and left it liable to the ordinary process of corruption. He asks:—

"Is what an idea historically becomes necessarily the true interpretation of it? The answer to this question, which may be derived from the history of religions, is a most emphatic No. Nothing is more conspicuous there than the tendency to deterioration, or the tendency on the part of a religion to change character by gradual self-accommodation to circumstances instead of moulding circumstances in accordance with its original idea" (pp. 205, 206).

He gives two instances: the one is Buddhism, the other is the rejection of Christ by the Jews.

"I draw from this a certain conclusion, namely, that a religion, because divinely inspired, is not therefore preserved from widespread deterioration; is not therefore prevented from receiving a development which, while it must appear as the chief historical development of the original, is in fact its parody."

He argues from Buddhism and Judaism to Christianity. I do not believe Buddhism to be divinely inspired, nor does Bishop Gore. I do not know that the Jews were promised the presence of the Holy Spirit until the end of the world, to lead them into all truth. I do not admit any strict parallel between the religion of the Old Testament and that of the New, for I do not admit their equality. Dr. Gore admits— every Christian must admit this much—that "the truth essential to make Christian saints has always been shining in the world through the witness of the Christian Church." He could not say less ! But he also admits "a possibility that the Church, short of substantial failure, may go far astray." (It appears from Dr. Gore's account that not much less than this has happened.) I do not wish to refute such remarks. I merely put two views side by side. Let the reader choose :

| "There is no guarantee that the Church may not, if she neglects the means provided to keep her right, get upon a false line of development, and that almost universally"(p. 207). | "I say unto thee, that thou art Peter, and upon this rock I will build My Church, and the gates of hell shall not prevail against it." |

But I will point out that

1. The second of these views, which is the Catholic view, and which I have given in the words of the Founder of the Catholic Church, does more honour to God. It represents Him as overruling the natural corruptions which overtake all natural religion, by a special grace and assistance, in order that the light may not fail by which men have to walk. According to Dr. Gore, those who follow Christ have often, nay, usually, to walk in the dimness of opinion, not in the light of faith.

2. This view makes us free with regard to history. We see the ship of the Church to-day sailing merrily over very rough water. How often has she seemed to suffer shipwreck ! Yet there she is, safe and sound. To investigate her past history is a most interesting, a most edifying study. The worse the scandals in the past, the greater the wonder of God's help that has made the Church survive. The Catholic historian can look difficulties in the face. He is not bound to any

theory of the past. He has the New Testament at the one end of the history and the Church of to-day at the other, both manifestly divine, and with an admittedly unbroken sequence binding the one to the other. How the development has taken place is a matter for critical examination, not for theorising.

Bishop Gore, on the contrary, is in a sad position. He appeals to history, and yet is bound hand and foot in discussing it. He is forced to admit that the development of the Papacy was practically necessary, was beneficial, was a part of a Divine plan ; but he is bound to find something "Satanic" in it to counteract these dangerous admissions. He is bound to find his favourite dogmas clearly expressed in early centuries, for he admits no real development. He is bound to find (somehow or other) antipapal difficulties and Roman corruptions. He goes to history with a theory, and he is lost if the facts cannot be strained to fit it. The majority of scholars do not think they can.

3. Our view makes the whole evolution which we trace in history an intelligible development. Bishop Gore makes it unintelligible. On his view the story of Christianity is a tangled web, a chaos of the inconsistent, the unexpected, the irrational. Take the evolution of Roman unity. To him this is the result of the Roman civil prestige, and of the Roman temper. It is a chance coincidence that Peter and Paul suffered in Rome. It is a chance that Rome alone of all the great Apostolic Churches has retained the faith unsullied through nineteen centuries. It is a chance that those who have been in communion with the Roman see have always immensely outnumbered any

other body of Christians. It is a chance that to-day Rome has half the Christian world united with one heart and one soul, and in one faith, in her obedience, over against the mutual discords and strifes which make Babel of the other half.

Is it, again, chance that Protestantism always ends in division and subdivision, because it has rejected unity? Was it a chance that those who fought against the Church in the sixteenth century were the immoral Luther, the cruel Calvin, the blasphemous Zwingli, the adulterous Beza, the lying and cowardly Cranmer, Henry, model of husbands, the virgin Elizabeth, and such like? Was it chance that those who defended unity were men like More and Fisher and Pole and Campion and Allen, or Ignatius and Charles Borromeo and Philip and Canisius? The lies of three hundred years are melting away like smoke before modern criticism, and we are beginning to know something of the men who robbed Englishmen of their faith by the use of rack and gibbet and cauldron. We know something of Foxe's martyrs now. We wish they had been kept from the stake, but we are forced to admit that most of them deserved the prison. But the white-robed army of martyrs tortured and slain by Henry and Elizabeth and the two Charleses is beginning to be known and respected by Protestant historians. We are learning how much we lost by the "Reformation." The crushing blow dealt to the universities, the loss of popular education throughout the country, scarcely at all made good by the scanty endowments of Edward VI., the wholesale destruction of libraries, the confiscation of the patrimony of the poor, the degradation of the clergy, the cessation of religious instruction, the beginning of vagrancy, the increase of immorality. If it had not been for the Puritans and John Wesley, there would have been little religion left in the country. Is all this chance?

Meanwhile, during three centuries, the great nations which remained Catholic — learned and civilised Italy, Spain and France only second to her—have had their day, as it seems. The younger half-barbarous peoples which fell a prey to the Protestant wolves are taking the first place in the world, and as each comes to the front it shakes off the slough of Protestantism. And rightly. No civilised people can be Protestant in the twentieth century, and Protestantism is doomed. But Christianity is not dead. If there is any vigorous life outside the ever-young Catholic Church, it is in the movements which have borrowed from her their spirit, it is in the men who have formed their lives on the models she offers them. Bishop Gore is of these. He has assimilated much. Will he not accept the whole?[1]

4. Our view gives us the spiritual help we need. The Church of England is a stepmother who neither teaches her children nor keeps them in order. We have a true Mother, "of her we are born, with her milk we are fed, with her

[1] Writing at Birmingham, I cannot avoid remarking that there are two rival bishops of Birmingham. A see was established here in 1850 by Pius IX. by his authority as the successor of St. Peter. In 1904 a rival see was set up by Edward VII. by his authority as successor of Queen Elizabeth. "Does any one think," says St. Cyprian, "that in one place there can be either many flocks or many pastors?" (*De Unit.*, 8.) Which is to be preferred? Which is in communion with the whole world?

spirit we are animated";[1] she teaches us, she governs us. We hear her voice as the voice of God, and we have Faith. We receive her Sacraments from birth to death, and we

[1] Cypr., *De Unit.*, 5.

have hope, confidence, perseverance. We enjoy through the Communion of Saints in her that union of charity of which it was said: "By this shall all men know that you are My disciples."

PLYMOUTH
WILLIAM BRENDON AND SON, LIMITED
PRINTERS